ALCTS Papers on Library Technical Services and Collections, #15

Perspectives on Serials
in the Hybrid Environment

HARRIET LIGHTMAN
and
JOHN P. BLOSSER
Editors

Association for Library Collections
& Technical Services

AMERICAN LIBRARY ASSOCIATION
Chicago   2007

Z
692
.S5
P477
2007

ALCTS Papers on Library Technical Services and Collections Series

SALSA de Tópicos = Subjects in SALSA: Spanish and Latin American Subject Access, #14
> Edited by David Miller and Filiberto Felipe Martínez Arellano, 90p. 2007, ALCTS. ISBN: 0-8389-8407-X

Managing Electronic Resources: Contemporary Problems and Emerging Issues, #13
> Edited by Pamela Bluh and Cindy Hepfer, 138p. 2006, ALCTS. ISBN: 0-8389-8366-9

Knowledge without Boundaries: Organizing Information for the Future, #12
> Edited by Michael A. Chopey, 96p. 2005, ALCTS. ISBN: 0-8389-8360-X

Marketing to Libraries for the New Millennium: Librarians, Vendors, and Publishers Review the Landmark Third Industry-Wide Survey of the Library Marketing Practices and Trends, #11
> Edited by Hendrik Edelman and Robert P. Holley, 216p. 2002, Scarecrow Press, Inc. ISBN: 0-8108-4271-8

Cataloging the Web: Metadata, AACR, and MARC 21, #10
> Edited by Wayne Jones, Judith R. Ahronheim, and Josephine Crawford, 208p. 2002, ScarecrowPress, Inc. ISBN: 0-8108-4143-6

Managing Electronic Serials, #9
> Edited by Pamela Bluh, 189p. 2001, ALA Editions. ISBN: 0-8389-3510-9

Virtually Yours: Models for Managing Electronic Resources and Services, #8
> Edited by Peggy Johnson and Bonnie MacEwan, 176p. 1998, ALA Editions. ISBN: 0-8389-0753-9

Bibliographic Control of Conference Proceedings, Papers, and Conference Materials, #7
> Edited by Olivia M. A. Madison and Sara Shatford Layne, 123p. 1996, ACRL. ISBN: 0-8389-7860-6

Future of the Descriptive Cataloging Rules, #6
> Edited by Brian E. C. Schottlaender, 135p. 1996, ALA Editions. ISBN: 0-8389-3477-3

Collection Management and Development: Issues in an Electronic Era, #5
> Edited by Peggy Johnson and Bonnie MacEwan, 148p. 1993, ALA Editions. ISBN: 0-8389-3447-1

Format Integration and Its Effect on Cataloging, Training, and Systems, #4
> Edited by Karen Coyle, 100p. 1993, ALA Editions. ISBN: 0-8389-3432-3

Collection Management for the 1990s, #3
> Edited by Joseph J. Branin, 178p. 1992, ALA Editions. ISBN: 0-8389-0608-7

Origins, Content, and Future of AACR2 Revised, #2
> Edited by Richard P. Smiraglia, 139p. 1992, ALA Editions. ISBN: 0-8389-3405-6

Subject Authorities in the Online Environment, #1
> Edited by Karen Markey, 84p. 1991, ALA Editions. ISBN: 0-8389-0558-7

Association for Library Collections & Technical Services (ALCTS)
ALCTS is a division of the American Library Association

ALCTS Publishing
50 E. Huron St.
Chicago, IL 60611
www.ala.org/alcts

Library of Congress Cataloging-in-Publication Data

Perspectives on serials in the hybrid environment / Harriet Lightman and
John P. Blosser, editors.
p.   cm. — (The ALCTS papers series ; #15)
Includes bibliographical references.
ISBN 0-8389-8415-0
1. Serials librarianship. 2. Libraries—Special collections—Serial publications.
3. Libraries—Special collections—Electronic journals. I. Lightman, Harriet.
II. Blosser, John P.
Z692.S5P47 2007
025.17'32—dc22   2006103086

Published in the United States of America.

Contents

Introduction

HARRIET LIGHTMAN AND
JOHN P. BLOSSER

For the past decade, if not longer, the shift from print to digital serials collections often has moved forward in fits and starts. This movement has unsettled the foundations of serials control and management—selecting, pricing, ordering, storing, and archiving—and spawned entirely new areas of expertise, most notably licensing. In some areas, such as law librarianship, the transition has been gradual, while in others, such as science, technology, and medicine (STM), the change has been swift and abrupt. At the same time, the demands of library users remain as varied as their choice of formats. Some patrons want only electronic serials, others prefer print, while still others demand both. Serials librarianship is rapidly evolving to match the dizzying challenges that come from changes in journal format and delivery. In this fast-paced environment, librarians must juggle user needs and expectations with vendor offerings while keeping a close watch on overall trends in their institutions and in librarianship in general.[1]

In all disciplines and library communities, staff who work with serials are adjusting standard operating practices and procedures to meet patron expectations for the seamless delivery of electronic materials. What are the current challenges and what lies ahead? Can librarians plan for the future, even if a degree of volatility is still the norm?[2]

Although the articles in this collection focus on university libraries, they describe some of the major issues that have consistently and tenaciously confronted all librarians in this hybrid environment. Several common themes related to serials management in general and to discipline-specific serials in particular are discussed. By sharing solutions as well as anxieties, the editors hope that order can be imposed on a complex and far-reaching topic and a dialogue can be initiated that will lead to creative solutions for both actual and anticipated problems.[3]

While these articles do not cover every aspect of serials control and management, they do offer a fresh approach to a number of complex subjects, including:

- archive, storage, and cancellation or retention of print serials;
- aggregators and the impact of bundling;
- pricing models, costs, and open access;
- assessment and use; and
- staffing and processing.

The first two essays in this book cut across disciplinary lines. In his overview of archiving and storage, John P. Blosser emphasizes the importance of license negotiation for archival rights and interlibrary loan, while also reminding readers to pay careful attention to any discrepancies between the print and electronic versions of particular titles before canceling print versions. His essay is accompanied by an annotated bibliography on this complex topic. In their description of the reorganization of technical services at the State University of New York at Buffalo, Cindy Hepfer, Susan Davis, and Daisy P. Waters take a similarly sweeping view of the immense complexities of negotiating between two environments as they sort out the difficulties of hiring, retaining, and training staff in this new setting.

Chapters three, four, and five focus on liberal arts and sciences and general reference serials. While Robert C. Michaelson, Anna Wu Ren, and Dana L. Roth concentrate on issues that are known to have the greatest impact on science and technology journals, they clearly suggest that science librarianship has taken a lead role in the shift from print to electronic formats.[4] In doing so, the authors identify some of the more worrisome aspects of managing electronic science serials, such as the impact of purchasing a package of titles—known colloquially as the big deal—as well as the lack of choice, content, and price. Harriet Lightman describes her attempts to evaluate several discipline-specific journal collections at Northwestern University. She focuses on evaluation methods for serials collections and discusses the viability of different techniques in an increasingly online environment. Jean M. Alexander depicts the rapidly mutating nature of reference serials and suggests some ways that librarians can manage this change in the short and long term. Her topics include selection and evaluation, storage and preservation, and problems unique to reference, such as the need to conduct annual collection reviews.

The final two essays concentrate on serials in libraries that have close links to both the academy and the professions, and provide a perspective on how libraries can accommodate the changes necessitated by the migration to electronic collections. Stephanie Schmitt, who concentrates on law serials management at Yale University's Lillian Goldman Law Library, underlines one of the unique complexities of law librarianship—the requirement that legal citations refer to print materials. Robin Klein, Patricia Hinegardner, Alexa Mayo, and Jane Murray discuss a range of ideas on health and medical librarianship using the University of Maryland's Health Sciences Library as a case study.

Archiving, Storage, and Cancellation or Retention of Print Serials

Scholars and librarians have always assumed that materials have a certain permanence: at best, a journal can be consulted on the shelf; at worst, on a microform reader. An article will always be where it should be, in an easily usable format, and accessible whenever the library is open. With the advent of electronic journal publishing, these certainties are vanishing. Some publishers have removed electronic content, while others have published electronic versions of serials that are different from their print counterparts. Students and scholars are unsure or uneasy about using electronic publications as journals of record and are confused about whether to cite the electronic or the print version of an article. This confusion applies equally to current and archival material. Access to electronic archives may depend on several factors, including regular payments to publishers and the stability and reliability of access mechanisms.

In an effort to alleviate the confusion and guarantee a more stable environment, librarians have begun to devise creative ways to house archival copies of journals in both print and electronic formats. Solutions such as Lots of Copies Keeps Stuff Safe (LOCKSS), the facsimiles provided by JSTOR, and the Portico project go a long way toward assuring scholars of the reliability of electronic archiving. However, as several of the articles in this collection point out, projects such as these are only a first step toward solving a massive problem.[5] Storing the print copies of journals with electronic versions is a particularly thorny problem for several reasons. Libraries that are short on space hesitate to invest time and money in preserving print journals if online versions exist. Yet print copies, especially older ones, may often have content that is not captured in their online counterparts. Where should these print copies be housed? Should they be stored in national or regional repositories? If so, how and by whom is access and preservation guaranteed? Who funds these print repositories, and what becomes of the copy of record? If an exact electronic facsimile is available, as in the case of JSTOR titles, is the copy-of-record question moot? And what about electronic articles that are not exact facsimiles of their print counterparts? In these latter cases, researchers and librarians may be faced with the critical task of identifying the copy of record. If the print version is the copy of record, what are the ramifications of canceling the print copy or removing the print volumes to a remote repository?[6]

Aggregators and the Impact of Bundling

Packaged electronic collections have a profound impact on many library areas. For the purposes of this volume, an *aggregator* is a single entity that provides electronic access to multiple journal titles. This single entity may be one company that provides electronic access to multiple journal titles by various publishers, associations, and other electronic journal providers (for example, LexisNexis Academic), or a company that provides electronic access to multiple journal titles published solely by one company (such as Elsevier's ScienceDirect). When an aggregated index database is acquired, librarians do not select individual titles. Rather, the mix of titles is based on license agreements the provider has with the publishers. In an aggregated database of titles from a single publisher, users are granted electronic access to current content and often to some backfile content as well. However, librarians are generally restricted from canceling print titles for the duration of the contract. Contracts of this type usually have a cap on price increases for annual renewals and often impede collection adjustment. Some single publisher packages may provide access to many titles that the library would not have selected individually. As a result, collection development is abandoned in lieu of collection management.[7]

When evaluating aggregations of titles, librarians should examine the following criteria:

- depth and breadth of content;
- pertinence of the content to the local collection;
- access method;
- interface functionality;
- bibliographic control through MARC record downloads or availability through link-resolver databases;

- package cost;
- customer and problem resolution services;
- management reports; and
- licensing terms, especially those allowing multiple-site access and document delivery options.

Because of the number and potential complexity of these criteria, a formal committee or informal group of interested parties from the collections, technical services, and information technology areas often weigh in on acquisition decisions.[8]

The economic viability of aggregated databases is circumstantial. Libraries may have the means to subscribe to several databases, and certainly in larger institutions, a greater variety of databases are needed and expected by the community. Yet, as libraries acquire multiple databases, content is frequently duplicated, and the library may be paying for the same content multiple times. Obviously, this situation cannot be sustained on an ongoing basis, and libraries should consider whether the cost of aggregated databases with large numbers of titles is worth the effort and expense of providing access to those titles. In addition, libraries should consider the potential impact of providing users with more content than may be needed for research purposes.

Pricing Models, Costs, and Open Access

Although the scholarly community is not completely reassured that print and electronic versions of a journal are identical, few libraries can afford the increasing demands of maintaining dual formats. While considerations of space must be taken into account, price is equally significant. Pricing models are complex and not uniform. Consortia deals, full time equivalent (FTE) pricing, subscription versus ownership, surcharges for print, and bundling by commercial publishers all lend to the confusion. Compounding the issue, libraries may find that by licensing aggregated packages, they are making titles available that would not have been individually selected. Moreover, as Michaelson, Ren, and Roth note, journals with low ISI impact factors are often bundled into a single package that cannot be cancelled under the terms of the contract. While Schmitt agrees that cost is a critical factor, she adds a note about the indispensable nature of some aggregators for legal research. Lightman adds yet another worrisome note when she speculates that the inclusion of such unwanted titles may dilute the integrity of a carefully selected, subject-specific collection. Can subject librarians truly know the cost of all journals in their subject areas if charges for unwanted titles are incorporated into bundled packages? And what are the hidden costs of subscribing to multiple electronic packages that may contain much duplication? Canceling print titles to pay for these large bundles may be a penny-wise solution to a large, unanalyzed problem. Open access titles, particularly those in the sciences, may in some cases help libraries gain access to scholarly content without impinging on the local budget. Because open access publishing is still rather new, the financial models that will define its longevity and reliability are still being worked out.[9]

Assessment and Use

How do librarians determine the audience for a particular journal or group of journals, and how do they measure the success of their title choices? In some fields, usage statistics are rapidly replacing more traditional means of journal evaluation. Science librarians, for example, continue to rely on ISI impact factors as well as usage statistics to gauge a journal's worth, while in some humanities disciplines, impact factors may be less relevant, usage statistics may be lacking, and traditional evaluation techniques may still be the most effective measure of a title's usefulness. How should new titles be chosen in a world where cost is king, titles are bundled, and libraries are often forced to choose between formats? Journal selection, as several of the authors in this volume point out, has often been driven by faculty requests. Perhaps new service models need to be considered by libraries that are used to having content readily available. Can a library continue to justify providing access to a journal that was requested and used by very few faculty members? What is to be done with a journal with very low usage? Would a pay-per-view or interlibrary lending model be acceptable if it were more cost effective than an annual subscription? Collection development is now less about choosing what to own than it is about choosing what to rent. In other words, collection development is shifting from ownership to access, a shift that most heavily impacts serials collections.[10]

Staffing and Processing

In a 2003 article, Ann Okerson painted a picture of librarians who bring traditional skills to the digital environment.[11] If these librarians are to succeed in organizing, preserving, and dispersing content, they will need to embrace change, adapt their traditional skill sets to work with new formats of information, and work together with colleagues both in the United States and abroad. Business as usual becomes impossible to define as workflows are changed and readjusted to handle acquisitions and access to electronic journals. Librarians used to a sizeable number of individual subscriptions find challenges in dealing with one package that may include hundreds of titles. Fortunately, librarians often use agents to help with ongoing subscription management, but establishing an initial list of titles is very time consuming. Staff must now have expertise with spreadsheets in order to organize subscription information. Accounting becomes complicated as costs are shared among subject funds and sometimes among libraries or schools within an institution or even among several autonomous institutions. Reducing the number of print subscriptions in favor of increasing online subscriptions in the belief that less physical processing will be required and that staff can be reduced is an erroneous assumption. Processing online resources is proving to be more complicated and time-consuming than processing print titles. Blosser sees some savings in traditional processing time at Northwestern University Library, but not to the extent that substantial hours may be reallocated to the processing of electronic resources. In many organizations, electronic resources licensing is now a standard component of acquisitions work. Depending on local regulations, licensing may add from a day to a month (or even more) to processing time. Skill in reading licenses and in negotiating license terms is now expected of a librarian involved in the acquisitions process, even if that person does not have signing authority. The challenge continues to be to re-engineer jobs to manage the online resources effectively.

Conclusion

The essays in this collection reflect the peculiarly chaotic, even topsy-turvy, nature of serials management and control in the ever-shifting online environment. Common worries are as present in this collection as are common themes. By identifying themes that cut across disciplinary lines, the editors hope that librarians will broaden their ongoing conversations about serials issues, share more concerns and practical considerations with their colleagues, and begin the long, steady process of creating new order out of chaos.

REFERENCE NOTES

1. Dees Stallings, "The Virtual University: Organizing to Survive in the 21st Century," *Journal of Academic Librarianship* 27, no. 1 (January 2001): 3–14; Association for Research Libraries Collections and Access Task Force, "Collections and Access for the 21st Century Scholar: Changing Roles of Research Libraries," *ARL Bimonthly Report* 225 (December 2002): 16.

2. Rick B. Forsman, "Managing the Electronic Resources Transforming Research Libraries: Challenges in the Dynamic Digital Environment," *Advances in Librarianship* 22 (1998): 1–19; Claire T. Dygert, "New Challenges behind the Scenes: The Changing Role of the Serials Librarian in the Age of E-publishing," *Internet Reference Services Quarterly* 3, no. 3 (1998): 7–14. Forsman points to a multitude of professional writings about the changes that took place in the mid-1990s, and offers some projections for the future of collections with electronic journals. Dygert reminds readers that the introduction of the Web as a distribution channel is what prompted an increase in and efficient distribution of journal material. Because access is no longer limited to users who are physically present in the library, librarians need to be familiar with a variety of access methods and proxy services. Title holdings, including backfiles, are easily updated online by the publisher, which dilutes the delineation of periodicity. Adding access to all of this content may be a challenge for serials catalogers as well (10–12).

3. It is impossible to keep up with the flood of new problems and solutions—there is a recent onslaught of literature on open access, for example, as well as literature on electronic journal management systems. Gary Ives ed., *Electronic Journal Management Systems: Experiences from the Field*, (Binghamton, N.Y.: Haworth, 2005); Charles A. Schwartz, "Reassessing Prospects for the Open Access Movement," *College & Research Libraries* 66, no. 6 (November 2005): 488–95; Pamela Bluh, "'Open Access,' Legal Publishing, and Online Repositories," *Journal of Law, Medicine & Ethics* 34, no. 1 (Spring 2006): 126–30. The *SPARC Open Access Newsletter* provides invaluable updates on open access issues. For example, the March 2006 issue contains details about Open J-Gate, a portal for open access to more than 3,000 journals. www.earlham.edu/~peters/fos/newsletter/03-02-06.htm (accessed 17 October 2006). Neil Jacobs ed., *Open Access: Key Strategic, Technical, and Economic Aspects* (Oxford: Chandos, 2006), www.eprints.org/community/blog/index.php?/archives/93-Open-Access-Key-Strategic-Technical-and-Economic-Aspects.html (accessed 17 October 2006).

4. Organisation for Economic Co-operation and Development, *Digital Broadband Content: Scientific Publishing* (Paris: OECD, 2005), www.oecd.org/dataoecd/42/12/35393145.pdf (accessed 10 April 2007). This report states that science publishing is key to research and distribution of research results. As many as three-quarters of scholarly journals are also available online. Scholarly publishers help incubate business models of online journal publishing, such as package deals and open access. The report goes on to state that integrating all types of digital publications for distribution presents a great challenge. Commercial and noncommercial efforts have been and will continue to be necessary to effectively deliver such information.

5. Karla Hahn, "Seeking a Global Perspective: Contributions from the U.K.," *ARL Bimonthly Report* 241 (August 2005): 9–10. Summary of a recent U.K. report on archiving that stresses self-archiving and open access.

6. In the case of legal research, the issue becomes even more labyrinthine because cited sources are either required or assumed to be to the print version. Deanna Marcum, "Requirements for the Future Digital Library," *Journal of Academic Librarianship* 29, no. 5 (September 2003): 276–79. Marcum notes that making library content available online anywhere is not necessarily easy or inexpensive, nor is it a call to collaborate, but it is nonetheless "a great and worthy goal." She maintains that libraries of the future will be comprehensive collections that are readily accessible and managed by "stewards of the intellectual and cultural heritages of the world"

(276). Marcum contends that libraries must collaborate to digitize the body of content needed to satisfy researchers' needs, despite of the dual obstacles of extended copyright restrictions and cost.

7. Curt Holleman, "Electronic Resources: Are Basic Criteria for the Selection of Materials Changing?" *Library Trends* 48, no. 4 (Spring 2000): 694.

8. Xiaotian Chen, "Figures and Tables Omitted from Online Periodical Articles: A Comparison of Vendors and Information Missing from Full-text Databases," *Internet Reference Services Quarterly* 10, no. 2 (2005): 75–88. Chen's article speaks to the difficulty of database selection and the real danger of losing content for users if only online versions are available.

9. Hahn, "Seeking a Global Perspective," 8–10; Schwartz, "Reassessing Prospects for the Open Access Movement." The open access model provides free access to journal content, but some interested parties are paying for the publication. In some cases, this responsibility may be assigned to the library, as Hahn discusses in a U.K. report on journal pricing that shows some surprising conclusions.

10. ARL, "Collections and Access for the 21st Century Scholar," 3, 5, 11. It is known that content that is available through the Web has more use by an expanding on-campus and remote population. There is also evidence that users expect complete journal runs to be available when needed.

11. Ann Okerson, "Asteroids, Moore's Law, and the Star Alliance," *Journal of Academic Librarianship* 29, no. 5 (September 2003): 280–85.

1 Issues of Archiving Content with an Eye toward the Future

JOHN P. BLOSSER

The preservation of both print and nonprint formats has been on the minds of librarians for some time. Archiving and storing both print and electronic journals is a massive, complicated, and nearly unmanageable task in the new hybrid library environment. For both formats, preservation efforts are intended to ensure the longevity of the content. With print, the emphasis is on the artifact, with the aim of keeping the physical artifact viable over many years. When dealing with electronic resources, the emphasis is on the carrier, the mode of transmission or distribution—CD-ROM, DVD, or more often, the Internet. To preserve the content of electronic resources, libraries and other repositories will need the technology to store and read this content now as well as in the future.

Simultaneously, with the ease of access, the introduction of electronic resources as part of a library's collection frequently results in redundancies in processing. Multiple entries for a title may be present in the catalog, possibly confusing users. Multiple payments may be required to account for the different formats, resulting in additional bookkeeping and record keeping. In addition, the acquisition of an electronic version also raises questions about the long-term preservation of both the print and electronic versions.

First and foremost, electronic journals provide a convenient form of access. It is important to realize, however, that they may not always replicate the printed versions in their entirety. In some cases, publishers provide only what they consider to be the core content of the journal in electronic form, including articles, reviews, submission guidelines, and news briefs. Because there is no standard for what is meant by *core content,* there may be considerable variations from one publisher to the next on what is included in e-journals. While this approach may be adequate for some disciplines, it is insufficient for many humanists and social scientists who need to examine the entire contents of the journal, even the advertisements. In some instances, the digital version may lack some of the content of the print version. In other cases, the digital content may include value-added features not available in the print format, such as inserted audio or video tracks, interactive manipulation of data for learning, or active links that illustrate a fresh, new concatenation of information on a subject. Differences between print and electronic versions raise questions about which version will be the journal of record in perpetuity.

The transition from print to digital is ongoing, making it difficult to predict the ultimate effect of electronic formats on information storage and reliability of access. While a publisher's assurance that content will be permanently available has been shown to be mostly reliable, it is not iron-clad. Some publishers have sold the rights to both the print and electronic versions of titles to other publishers, so that, in at least a modest number of cases, a library may no longer access the online archives of a title to which it had been guaranteed access by a license agreement with a former publisher. License negotiation is crucial on this point. When negotiating a license for archival access, librarians should insist on contractual guarantees to perpetual archival access in the event that the publisher changes or otherwise ceases to maintain the content.

Ongoing access to online content is also dependent on the ready availability of appropriate technology. A number of efforts are underway to archive digital content, such as JSTOR: The Scholarly Journal Archive, Lots of Copies Keep Stuff Safe (LOCKSS), the University Licensing Program (TULIP), OCLC's Electronic Collections Online, e-Depot, and Portico.[1] In order to guarantee accessibility, some publishers, such as Blackwell Publishing, Elsevier, and Oxford University Press, have made arrangements to have content hosted at multiple sites.

Numerous different licensing arrangements exist for electronic resources. Libraries may buy archival content and mount the files locally on their own servers, or they may lease access to content housed on the publishers' servers. Other publishers make archival content available only as long as a library maintains a print subscription to the current content. With widespread availability and increased popularity of electronic journals, questions of retention and preservation of print material have mushroomed. Each library must plan a course of action based on the needs of its students, faculty, and community users; the budget that may be allocated toward the archiving solution; and any consortia or regional cooperation that may be available for sharing the costs and creating and maintaining the necessary infrastructure. Should the library retain the print material and if so, should it be retained onsite or stored off-site? Could the print materials be withdrawn and discarded?

Identifying sufficient space for expanding print collections is a concern frequently voiced by many librarians. If the library provides online access to the content of some journals, what are the arguments for retaining the print counterparts? Is there artifactual value in the print version? Do faculty insist on using it because of convenience or for instructional purposes? If print materials are removed are there print copies available at other libraries within a reasonable travel radius? Or can stable online access to archived content be guaranteed? Is timely delivery through interlibrary loan an option? Most libraries are still acquiring new print materials, so providing adequate shelf space is important. Would the removal of print material help to make room for new receipts? Regional or national print repositories or shared storage facilities are a welcome means of preserving content and may be an option for libraries that require shelf space in order to satisfy an active acquisitions program. Participants in these repositories usually find it advisable to collaborate on collection development, so that not every library must retain every print title in perpetuity.

When migrating from a largely print collection to one that is primarily electronic, the needs of interlibrary loan must also be taken into account. As print collections are discontinued, stored off-site, and no longer readily accessible, libraries rely more and more on electronic versions to fulfill interlibrary loan requests. Currently most license agreements allow lending libraries to print content and then mail or fax the information to the requesting library. Some agreements allow the content to be printed and then scanned to a digital format in order to be securely transmitted by such software as Ariel or Odyssey that also limits the number of views or downloads of the material.[2] However, agreements that allow libraries to satisfy interlibrary loan requests by electronically providing requested items are not yet universally accepted. As technology advances to allow a secure transmission of content that earns the trust of publishers and authors and protects their commercial investment and proprietary rights, librarians dedicated to efficiently fulfilling the collection needs of their users hope that it will soon be acceptable to electronically transmit journal content directly from the online version to the user, thereby revolutionizing interlibrary loan.

The Costs of Archiving

Online content may be provided in a number of different configurations and pricing models. Some publishers offer subscribers access to current and archival material at a single price, others may offer combinations of current and archival access according to a sliding fee scale, and still others may include access to archival material as long as a current subscription to the print version is maintained. If digital content is hosted locally, such overhead expenses as hardware and software maintenance must also be considered. While consortium purchases are often cost-effective because they make it possible for libraries to acquire resources that they might otherwise not be able to afford, there may be added costs associated with consortial access. Whatever the fiscal arrangements, libraries need to be confident that the content they license will remain available to all authorized users throughout the life of the contract. Of equal concern is the need to maintain software for accessing, searching, and viewing digital archives that is readily upgradeable or provides users with a trustworthy migration path if new software is required

Although a library may invest heavily in building an electronic collection, this does not mean that it will automatically give up its print collections. However, it is important to keep in mind that there will be ongoing costs associated with the maintenance of both formats for many years to come. These include overhead costs related to processing, housing, shelving, and preserving the physical items as well as costs related to interlibrary lending. Libraries may believe that constructing new space or renovating an existing facility will solve their space problems. Such a plan requires a significant investment due to the high cost of construction, and consequently, it is rarely a viable option. Regardless of the type of facility a library maintains, ongoing costs for a variety of management and operational activities, such as inventory control and maintaining or adhering to industry standards for environmental control and disaster preparedness, will be incurred. Libraries must also take into account the expenses related to circulation, interlibrary loan, and document delivery. Even if libraries from one institution or one regional or consortium endeavor share a print repository, participating libraries must take into account the costs that will have to be shouldered by one or several of the stakeholders.

Conclusion

Libraries have embraced the need for electronic content, but long-term accessibility and availability of this content is a topic of vital concern to authors, publishers, and librarians. There is no single archiving model that is workable for every library. It has been helpful that different models have been initiated and tested with the participation of libraries and publishers. While newer models may have appealing archiving advantages over previous models, they may still have elements that make them inappropriate in some instances. The archiving of electronic content needs to continue to evolve, and it is implicit that viable delivery mechanisms can be developed that will allow the content to be readily migrated to new and improved storage devices, thereby keeping the content alive and useable for future generations.

Literature Review

Archiving content is a centuries-old discussion. Models of archiving electronic content continue to be discussed and developed. This annotated bibliography will give readers a sense of the issues related to archiving in the digital age together with a few references to print archiving. As new formats must be archived, the discussion needs to expand to encompass the transition from physical carriers to delivery and storage of electronic content.

Arora, Jagdish. "Building Digital Libraries: An Overview." *DESIDOC Bulletin of Information Technology* 21, no. 6 (2001): 3–24.

Arora outlines efforts to build digital collections, listing technology developments and the shift to allow communication among various information systems. Digital libraries encompass different categories of resources that affect how they are stored and accessed: content written in legacy software, content that will transition to different software, and content that will be changed to new and future software. Arora discusses ways in which libraries might build digital collections, but indicates that libraries will purchase access to many resources rather than acquiring the resources locally. The publication includes a good overview of the technology issues involved in providing access to an archive of resources, including steps in the digitization process.

Cain, Mark. "Being a Library of Record in a Digital Age." *Journal of Academic Librarianship* 29, no. 6 (2003): 405–10.

The preservation of traditional materials in digital form has much promise, but the preservation of the digital form for reuse in the future may be problematic. Cain uses the Web as an example. The author reviews methods of digital preservation: capturing and storing the technology to use the digital content; emulating the technology to access and use the content; moving content to updated formats and platforms, which may lead to data and formatting loss; and, persistent object preservation that describes the original digital properties. Choices of standards of digital replication sometimes need to be made. One standard widely accepted is the Open Archival Information System (OAIS), which addresses digital preservation issues from the creation of the content to storage of the content in the repository. Cain describes a number of efforts at digital preservation by publishers, national libraries and governmental agencies, foundations and research libraries, and nonprofit organizations.

Day, Michael. "Digital Preservation and Long-term Access to the Content of Electronic Serials." In *E-Serials: Publishers, Libraries, Users, and Standards*, 2nd ed., 167–95. New York: Haworth, 2003.

Day compares the assessment of the electronic journal to the same parameters used to evaluate the traditional print peer-reviewed journal. He briefly outlines early efforts between libraries and publishers to disseminate content to users. The author reports on efforts of self-archiving, drawing on such examples as the Los Alamos National Laboratory preprints and the U.S. National Institutes of Health PubMed Central. Day also lists the pros and cons of various electronic journal distribution methods and formats. He delineates some problems with long-term storage of electronic media and proposes preservation strategies while addressing the issue of lasting authenticity or integrity of the content and the importance of maintaining accurate dates for different versions of the content. Day discusses how various individuals or groups could take responsibility for digital preservation and describes three models for digital preservation: a decentralized approach by the author or creator of the content, a centralized approach by national and larger research libraries, and a combination of the two approaches. Day concludes that preservation efforts will likely be achieved through cooperation among the various interested parties.

Drake, Miriam A. "Science, Technology, and Information." *Journal of Academic Librarianship* 27, no. 4 (2001): 260–62.

Since the mid-1940s, the growth in scientific information has been phenomenal, and, as it continues to expand, better management, description, organization, and dissemination are required. Who will manage and store this information? Will there be a document of record if content can be modified online? Authenticity and documentation of experiments are important to scientists, and preservation is central to the future of scientific investigation. New generations of scientists are familiar with networked, global information sources and expect to find more historical documentation online to facilitate their research. At the same time, they are often unaware of the costs associated with providing online resources. Drake states that in the future, effective library services will be centered around the librarian, and not the library building.

Edwards, Eli. "Ephemeral to Enduring: The Internet Archive and Its Role in Preserving Digital Media." *Information Technology and Libraries* 23, no. 1 (2004): 3–8.

Edwards cites statistics about the short-lived nature of a fairly large percentage of Internet sites. Although there is no central archiving effort, national libraries have initiated models of archiving national content, both official and unofficial. Edwards writes about the Internet Archive (IA), a project begun in 1996 by Alexa Internet, now wholly owned by Amazon.com. IA has a variety of collection divisions, including Web sites, multimedia, and digitized content. Access is free and was enhanced to include older files with the Wayback Machine, a search engine that recreates links within its own database, providing links to Web pages stored within its archives. IA has developed procedures to preserve content as well as maintain systems of access as technology changes. In addition, IA directors have had to deal with copyright issues. Although IA is an extensive Web archive, it does not function as a library because it lacks indexing and classification and has no keyword searching capability. Edwards compares the IA with a number of library projects designed to archive the Internet.

Hill, J. B., Cherie Madarash-Hill, and Nancy Hayes. "Remote Storage of Serials: Its Impact on Use." *Serials Librarian* 39, no. 1 (2000): 29–39.

Due to overcrowding of traditional materials, libraries turn to remote storage facilities, on or off campus, and sometimes take part in a regional storage effort. Using the University of Akron Science and Technology Library as an example, the authors describe the planning process for a storage facility and the moving of material to such a facility. They also provide an evaluation of a remote storage facility, listing issues regarding decisions, characteristics, and the pros and cons relating to remote storage.

Hodge, Gail. "Preservation of and Permanent Access to Electronic Information Resources: A System Perspective." *Information Services & Use* 25 (2005): 47–57.

Hodge puts the discussion of archiving and preservation requirements within the framework of the concepts and terminology of the OAIS reference model, pointing out that archiving should be considered when the content is created and published so that formats are consistent with archiving means. Newly purchased content will be migrated into an archive, and the system requirements should allow that to happen easily. Descriptive metadata must record the origin of the first version of the content as well as subsequent versions in such a way that this information can be reproduced in future technologies. The archiving community is discussing the appropriate format for archiving. Should a master archive be established in case of need, while an archive in a different format is used for dissemination of content? Hodge explains the preservation strategies of migrating content to new hardware and software and emulating original hardware and software by including coding that instructs new technology on how to handle the data. The author provides a brief history of several archiving systems, including Digital Information Archive System (DIAS); OCLC Digital Archive; PANDORA Digital Archiving System (PANDAS); Lots of Copies Keep Stuff Safe (LOCKSS); Dspace Institutional Digital Repository System; Flexible Extensible Digital Object Repository Architecture (Fedora); and Portable PubMed Central. While efforts continue to refine standards among and between systems, the cost of archiving and the development of sustainable business models may prove to be more difficult challenges.

International Federation of Library Associations and Institutions. "IFLA Statement on Open Access to Scholarly Literature and Research Documentation." *IFLA Journal* 30, no. 1 (2004): 59–60.

The statement, adopted by the IFLA governing board on December 5, 2003, outlines IFLA's seven principles on open access. Principle number 7 addresses issues of long-term preservation and availability of research literature in digital form.

Jaguszewski, Janice M., and Laura K. Probst. "The Impact of Electronic Resources on Serials Cancellations and Remote Storage Decisions in Academic Research Libraries." *Library Trends* 48, no. 4 (2000): 799–820.

Jaguszewski and Probst consider traditional and new criteria with which to evaluate the cancellation of print serials, the role of electronic resources on cancellation decisions, and how these criteria impact the decision to store print serials at sites that are remote from the physical library's collection. Traditional criteria are taken from the *Guide to Review of Library Collections* (American Library Association, 1991), and include use; subscription price; coverage in indexing and abstracting services; availability; subject coverage, intellectual level; future programmatic value; and duplication of formats or access. New criteria include availability of network mechanics and support; quality and functionality of the user interface; licensing considerations; competition among vendors; consortia arrangements; and archiving options. The authors also discuss the criteria used to select print materials being considered for storage. In addition to three traditional guidelines—ready user access, space requirements for growing collections, and protection of specific materials—the authors consider a number of other criteria: economics of building digital collections; cultural and organizational views of using digital collections; user expectations and skills to access electronic format; copyright for local, remote, and lending use; and the need for archiving and the associated issues of future platform migrations, maintenance costs, and determining authenticity. Jaguszewski and Probst assess criteria for storage in regards to availability of electronic resources, including actual use, projected use, protective storage and physical condition, duplication, and availability.

Kenney, Anne R., and others. "E-Journal Archiving Metes and Bounds: A Survey of the Landscape." *CLIR Publications* 138 (September 2006). Accessed 16 October 2006 www.clir.org/PUBS/abstract/pub138 abst.html.

Using a method similar to an early land-surveying measurement scheme called metes and bounds, the report considers seven aspects of archiving e-journals: mission and mandate, rights and responsibilities, content coverage, minimal services, access rights, organizational viability, and network. The report shows that the archiving landscape has room for development, but it is becoming more conducive to participation by academic libraries, and there are several "viable choices for exercising good digital stewardship." Together with publishers and archiving agents, academic libraries must take a proactive role to make this a successful effort.

Lynch, Clifford A. "Digital Library Opportunities." *Journal of Academic Librarianship* 29, no. 2 (2003): 286–89.

Lynch calls for grassroots action to prepare libraries for the future. He looks at changes in scholarly communication facilitated by digital technology and the role the author may play in the process. Libraries facilitate scholarly communication and offer a "safety net both for access and preservation." Critical editions of scholarly research will need to be reconceptualized in digital format, not just digitized. Readers will be not only humans but various kinds of programs that find and manipulate data. Digital libraries are built from digital collections and a community of users. People should be flexible in defining the digital library and strive to span the three realms of digital information: personal, organizational, and public.

———. "Institutional Repositories: Essential Infrastructure for Scholarship in the Digital Age." *ARL: A Bimonthly Report on Research Library Issues and Actions from ARL, CNI, and SPARC* 226 (February 2003), 1–7 Accessed 14 March 2007, www.arl.org/resources/pubs/br/br226/br226ir.shtml.

Recent technological advances are making online storage more affordable, and standards are making content more uniformly accessible. Some efforts toward open access are making scholarly information free to the public. Lynch defines an institutional repository not only as a set of services for accessing content but more importantly, as "an organizational commitment to the stewardship" of digital documents with preservation, access, and distribution. Committing to a repository is a realization that scholarship will be more and more dependent on documents in a digital format. The institutional repository will complement, not replace, traditional forms of scholarship. Lynch cautions readers about some pitfalls to establishing an institutional repository: administrative control over intellectual content, loading policy constraints on the infrastructure, and building hastily and without a committed purpose. The author believes institutional repositories can help develop standards for networking information and the underlying infrastructure regarding preservation of formats, content identifiers, and rights management.

Machovec, George. "Preservation of Digital Resources." In *Managing Electronic Resources: Contemporary Problems and Emerging Issues*, ed. by Pamela Bluh and Cindy Hepfer, ALCTS Papers on Library Technical Services and Collections, no. 13. Chicago: Association for Library Collections & Technical Services, 2006, 110–17.

Digital resources create new challenges for preservation not experienced with print materials, including the ease with which content can be removed from the resource, as has been seen most frequently when the U.S. government has removed material it deems sensitive. The obsolescence of hardware and software poses special challenges, particularly because the longevity of electronic storage media is not known. Changing copyright laws may also affect access to digital media. Machovec asks "who is responsible for the preservation of digital data?" The role of the library in preserving print has been a time-honored model, but preserving digital data is different. Rather than owning the content, as they did in the past, libraries now often lease access to digital content. In order to answer the question of who is responsible for archiving digital resources, much more discussion and planning will be needed. Publishers, libraries, and users need to work together to establish the best methods for long-term data storage and access. Machovec reports on the framework for building reliable, long-term digital collections under the auspices of the Institute of Museum and Library Services and suggests that much work will be needed in order to develop viable solutions to digital archiving.

Marcum, Deanna B. "Research Questions for the Digital Era Library." *Library Trends* 51, no. 4 (2003): 636–51.

This article addresses three questions, the second of which is devoted to preservation planning for digital and traditional resources. Marcum declares that more research is needed in both areas because they should be considered together for effective preservation programming. She outlines a number of major programs in support of preservation throughout the 1980s and 1990s, many of which were devoted to the preservation of traditional materials. The library profession as a whole needs to establish a clearer vision of digital resource preservation. As new digital resources are created, the need to include them in a preservation strategy is crucial. Marcum delineates past actions by preservation subthemes: the state of preservation programs, covering such issues as library trends, digital development, existing benchmarks as applied to future applications, national leadership, education and recruitment, collaboration, and economics; how best to preserve digital materials, and how a Library of Congress project, along with other independent projects, is providing direction; and how to improve preservation of traditional materials and what choices are necessary to select what will be digitized for preservation.

McClaren, Mary. "Current Library Collection Storage Models." *Kentucky Library Association* 68, no. 1 (2004): 15–20.

Recognizing the need for user space in academic libraries today, McClaren uses the University of Kentucky Libraries as a starting point for her white paper on storage models in use at universities. Four shelving types are described: stationary, compact movable, low- or high-rise industrial, and rack with bin-type containers. These storage areas may be built within a library or at remote sites on or off campus. The facilities are environmentally controlled to provide optimum temperature and humidity for long-term storage of traditional materials. McClaren compares the high-density book shelving system (HDBSS, or Harvard model) and the automated storage and retrieval system (ASRS), and references cost comparisons in building and ongoing maintenance.

Moorthy, A. Lakshmana, and C. R. Karisiddappa. "Mass Storage Technologies for Libraries and Information Centers." *DESIDOC Bulletin of Information Technology* 20, no. 5 (2000): 3–20.

The authors contend that expanding print collections influenced the development of digital storage of library materials. Mass storage provides large-volume archival management, access to the growing volume of information in digital format, access to multimedia data, and networking of data between systems. The authors give brief, technical overviews of various magnetic and optical storage technologies for both document and multimedia data, from various uses of magnetic tape to different formats of DVDs, and conclude with some future trends.

O'Connor, Phyllis. "Remote Storage Facilities: An Annotated Bibliography." *Serials Review* 20, no. 2 (1994): 17–44.

This bibliography offers documents with valuable background information on issues related to storage facilities for traditional materials and includes works on the planning process, the facility, selecting materials for storage, and implementation of the storage program.

Peters, Thomas A. "Digital Repositories: Individual, Discipline-based, Institutional, Consortial, or National?" *Journal of Academic Librarianship* 28, no. 6 (2002): 414–17.

Interest in institutional repositories is fueled by faculty self-archiving, objections by libraries to the journal publishing system, and the introduction of more sophisticated technology to network and publish digital content. Whether the organizational structure of the repository is individual, discipline-based, institutional, consortial, or national, it is not as important as the fact that the content is digital. Peters briefly defines the term *repository,* gives examples of institutional and consortial repositories, and offers the pros and cons of library participation in consortial digital repositories.

Stemper, Jim, and Susan Barribeau. "Perpetual Access to Electronic Journals: A Survey of One Academic Research Library's License." *Library Resources & Technical Services* 50, no. 2 (April 2006): 91–100.

Using many examples of license clauses for electronic journal access, Stemper and Barribeau discuss the need to negotiate access to subscribed online content in the event that the content is sold to another publisher, the publisher goes out of business, or the subscriber no longer subscribes to the online content. Perpetual access is a topic that must be included in ongoing negotiations between the provider and the subscriber of online content.

Tennant, Roy. "Coping with Disasters." *Library Journal* 126, no. 19 (2001): 26–28.

Planning and preparation may minimize damage. Prevention may mitigate damage or prevent it from occurring in the first place. Protecting digital systems depends on the storage architecture of the data, availability of a consistent power supply, physical access to hardware security, backup copies stored at safe distances, and the use of mirroring sites. Tennant recommends the *Emergency Management Guide for Business and Industry*, published by the Federal Emergency Management Administration as a place to start planning.

Teper, Thomas H., and Beth Kraemer. "Long-term Retention of Electronic Theses and Dissertations." *College & Research Libraries* 63, no. 1 (2002): 61–72.

By addressing the retention of electronic theses and dissertations, the authors touch on preservation issues related to the electronic format. Preservation activity is termed asset management. Long-term access and preservation go hand-in-hand. Access to content may be preserved in cases where the artifact itself is not saved. The authors discuss the semantic differences of the phrase *digital preservation*. There is flexibility in the access methods of digital materials, but the development of software occurs so rapidly that long-term planning of digital preservation is difficult. Teper and Kraemer briefly mention digital preservation models, such as migration, emulation, analog backups, and container storage, and outline a number of efforts to make storage and delivery of original content more reliable for the future.

Terrio, Robert. "Electronic Metaphors and Paper Realities." *Progressive Librarian* 21 (Winter 2002): 28–37.

> Terrio compares the copyright environment for print material to the contract environment for electronic resources. The author suggests several options for licensing agreements that would be amenable to libraries, yet fair to all parties, and points out the risks involved in only licensing material in an electronic format. Terrio discusses collection development and how the acquisition of electronic resources impacts collection decisions in light of budget restrictions. Turning to archiving issues, Terrio writes that access rather than ownership may be the future of libraries. While he indicates that storage and preservation are necessary for both print and electronic resources, he questions whether the technology to read particular electronic formats will be available in the future.

Thomas, Sarah. "From Double Fold to Double Bind." *Journal of Academic Librarianship* 28, no. 3 (2002): 104–108.

> Thomas discusses the growth of preservation efforts and suggests that, even in the digital age, print is still popular as a reliable archival source. All parties agree on the importance of preserving digital copies of journals, but who is best suited to assume the responsibility? The author lists the qualities, requirements, and framework that make for a strong and reliable digital repository.

Watson, Paula D. "Who Will Keep Print in the Digital Age? Current Thinking on Shared Repositories." In *Managing Electronic Resources: Contemporary Problems and Emerging Issues*, ed. by Pamela Bluh and Cindy Hepfer, ALCTS Papers on Library Technical Services & Collections, no. 13. Chicago: Association for Library Collections & Technical Services, 2006, 118–32.

> There is a tension in preserving multiple formats that is mostly due to the cost of both archiving print serials and leasing access to the same content online. Some libraries would like to do the latter and leave print archiving to larger and perhaps higher-profile institutions. Understandably, print archives provide security for retaining content for the future. Watson describes efforts toward national shared print repositories, citing the JSTOR project as an example. At the same time, development of long-term electronic archiving is moving ahead. JSTOR materials are being used "to test a framework for the distributed, long term retention of artifactual collections" in a project funded by the Mellon Foundation and coordinated by the Center for Research Libraries. Assembling

complete print runs in good condition can be expensive and problematic, as was demonstrated by the Research Collections and Preservation Consortium (ReCAP) project. Merging collections to build one single archive collection means libraries must share ownership of the archive and de-duplicate their collections. Watson cites the University of California system and the Five College Library Depository in the Northeast as examples of "promising models" for print repositories. She suggests that in the future there may be specialized repositories coordinated on the regional or national level, some of which would have unique copies of materials, while others would contain materials of artifactual value, and still others may consist of the "collections of record."

Wiggins, Richard. "Digital Preservation: Paradox and Promise." Netconnect, *Library Journal*.com (April 15, 2001): 12–15. Accessed 8 March 2007, www.libraryjournal.com/article/CA106209.html.

Using the White House Web site as an example, Wiggins postulates that information may be born digital, be accessible through the Internet, and then disappear from the Web. Reasons for content loss may include: overwriting old content with new updates; redesigning a site; changing a sponsor, or sponsor's intent; losing functionality due to software changes; changing storage media and software formats; and disasters that destroy data not adequately secured or stored. Although digital storage costs are low, and storing content digitally may help preserve the content and extend its availability, other costs, such as rights management, may add to the expense of digital preservation. Obsolescence of software and hardware may result in losing digitally stored content, and efforts to preserve or emulate the reading software or proactively migrate the content and applications to new technology need to be considered.

Zeichick, Alan. "Building a Dam to Last: Archiving Digital Assets." *EContent* 26, no. 5 (2003): 40-46.

Written from the perspective of a business application, this article outlines steps to consider when planning to protect an organization's digital assets, including identifying the assets and assessing their potential value to the organization and to the users of the product; determining how access to the content will be achieved; and establishing the appropriate software architecture. Given content creation, publication, and delivery needs, systems need to be built to maintain archives as well as to integrate new creations into them. Zeichick raises the question of how much content to archive, citing the 80/20 rule of usage and need, and suggests that it may be advantageous to store some content in multiple formats to minimize the time needed to translate the content into different programs.

REFERENCE NOTES

1. Established in 1995 as an independent nonprofit organization, JSTOR (www .jstor.org/) digitizes content from journals that are widely subscribed to, frequently represented in citation analysis, have a lengthy publishing history, and are recommended by experts in the journal's discipline. The JSTOR model provides subscription access to content from the beginning volume up to a point at which the subscriber must also subscribe to the current volumes through the publisher. JSTOR adds one year to the archive each year as part of the moving wall of content model.

   In testing and beta versions since 1999, Lots of Copies Keep Stuff Safe, or LOCKSS (www.lockss.org/lockss/Home), was released into production in 2004 by Stanford University. The model is one of multiple copies of online journal content stored digitally by several participating library members. LOCKSS is open source software that manages digital content delivered through the Web to be stored on a PC hard drive. The member networked PCs communicate with each other to verify that full copies of the content are being maintained.

   The University Licensing Program, or TULIP (www.elsevier.com/wps/find/ authored_newsitem.cws_home/companynews05_0002), was an experiment in providing locally archived online journal content. Elsevier worked with nine U.S. university libraries between 1991 and 1995. Though discontinued, the experiment exposed important technology issues in the delivery and access of online journals.

   Electronic Collections Online, or ECO (www.oclc.org/electroniccollections/), is a subscription service from OCLC accessed through the OCLC search interface called FirstSearch. ECO is a growing collection of more than 5,000 journals that can be selected, managed, and archived to meet the individual library's collection needs.

   Developed in close cooperation between IBM and Koninklijke Bibliotheek (KB), the National Library of the Netherlands, e-Depot (www.kb.nl/dnp/e-depot/e-depot-en.html) has been in operation from early 2003. The software works as a harvester of online content of publishers who have signed an agreement to participate in the archive. The archive software is also structured to allow the transition to newer software as it develops to maintain a viable permanent archive.

   Portico (www.portico.org/) grew out of the Electronic-Archiving Initiative of JSTOR in 2002. In 2004, the archive became part of Ithaka Harbors and was launched into production in 2005. Publishers and libraries can participate in the archive as subscribing members. The digital files store the content of the journal titles submitted by publishers in a format that can be easily migrated to new software as it is developed in the future. The archive is meant to be a repository of content that is not used until a time when digital files are no longer supplied by a publisher. (All accessed 17 June 2006.)

2. Ariel (www4.infotrieve.com/products_services/ariel.asp) is a document transmission system that "allows users to send electronic images to other Ariel workstations anywhere in the world . . . and converts them to PDF files for easy patron delivery. This service is faster and clearer than a fax . . . and handles the most detailed images."

Odyssey (www.atlas-sys.com/products/odyssey/) electronic delivery software "allows for the transmission and receipt of electronic documents between other Odyssey sites, sites using OCLC ILLiad, and sites using other software packages that implement the Odyssey protocol. It uses the standard TWAIN scanner drivers that come with most scanners and works with black and white, grayscale, color, or any combination of these scanned formats. Upon receipt, the documents can be printed, automatically converted to PDF format, or saved in the original TIF format." (All accessed 17 June 2006.)

Transforming Technical Services Units to Accommodate Electronic Resource Management

CINDY HEPFER, SUSAN DAVIS,
AND DAISY P. WATERS

In the mid-1990s, during the early days of remote electronic access to scholarly materials, two schools of thought prevailed in academic libraries. The first was to dive in headfirst and go electronic as quickly and completely as possible, while the second—and more common approach—was to be cautious and see whether electronic periodicals would develop critical mass and standardized access options. Within the last decade, there has been a dramatic change in the way libraries view electronic publications. Users in all types of libraries, but especially in academic libraries, have become addicted to the Internet as a means to discover and access content. Moreover, they now expect that remote access materials will be available twenty-four hours a day, seven days a week. Recognizing the burgeoning demand for electronic versions, both large and small publishers and aggregators developed their own platforms or made arrangements to outsource the provision of the electronic version. No matter how they did it, publishers and aggregators quickly made a huge number of scholarly and popular publications available through the Web. Librarians—even those who had been dragging their feet—began to purchase or lease access to ever larger numbers of electronic resources. They also began to actively campaign for acceptable license terms, reasonable pricing models, and various forms of permanent archival access.

Within a decade, electronic journals and other e-resources have become of paramount importance to many, if not most, academic libraries. An article by Kyrillidou and Young, based on a 2003–2004 survey of Association of Research Libraries (ARL) member institutions, indicates that the growth rate of expenditures for electronic materials far exceeded those for library materials in general among the largest scholarly and research collections in North America.[1] In fact, the data showed that in each of the preceding ten years, expenditures for e-resources in ARL libraries grew between three and ten times faster than total materials expenditures. By 2003–4, the average ARL library was spending more than 31 percent of its materials budget on electronic resources, with fourteen libraries spending more than half of their materials budgets on electronic materials. Based on the findings outlined in the report, it is clear that electronic resources have become a fact of life.

The increase in the acquisition of electronic versions of scholarly and popular materials in all types and sizes of libraries has prompted significant and often abrupt changes to both services and collections. Libraries that expend a considerable portion of their acquisitions budget on electronic resources frequently dedicate substantial staff resources and effort in guiding users to these often high-priced materials. In some cases, systems staff who are intensely occupied with many other critical duties have had to assume new e-resource-related responsibilities, such as overseeing a proxy server, implementing and maintaining linking services, and responding to reports of electronic resource misuse or abuse. Reference and bibliographic instruction librarians have turned much of their attention from teaching patrons how to use printed finding aids to offering instruction on how to locate and access electronic versions of articles, books, images, and data sets. Collections staff are dealing with new issues and concepts in relation to selection, deselection, and weeding. Technical services staff have had to accept responsibility for the acquisition, cataloging, and ongoing management of e-resources while simultaneously continuing to acquire and organize traditional library materials. Meanwhile, the workload has declined in a few areas. For example, circulation departments are checking out fewer materials and consequently, fewer materials require reshelving; acquisitions departments are acquiring fewer monographs; and cataloging departments are cataloging fewer books. The information environment has changed so quickly and dramatically that many libraries have had to cope with the new demands on the fly, rather than carefully and sequentially planning how to revise the workflow and reorganize staff.

This paper presents information about a reorganization of technical services at one ARL-member institution, the State University of New York at Buffalo, and highlights the creation of a new department to handle electronic periodicals and databases. This paper also outlines concepts that administrators and supervisors might consider in reorganizing for electronic resource management.

Background

The University of Buffalo was founded in 1846 as a private medical college. In 1962 it merged with the State University of New York (SUNY) system and became the State University of New York at Buffalo, also known as the University at Buffalo (UB). It is the flagship of the sixty-four-campus SUNY system. While the director of libraries, whose title is associate vice president for university libraries, reported to the vice president and chief information officer for several years, the director currently reports to both the provost and the executive vice president for finance and operations. Approximately 180 librarians, professional, and clerical staff work in the university libraries.[2] The libraries consist of an architecture and planning library, a graduate library, an undergraduate library, and a science and engineering library that form the arts and sciences libraries (ASL); the health sciences library (HSL); the law library; the music library; the university archives, the poetry collection, and rare books which together form special collections; an office of Web development; the microcomputer support office; systems; an educational technology center; and, of course, administration. Until January 2005, the central technical services (CTS) and technical services departments in HSL and the law library supported library operations.

In 2003–2004, the UB libraries reported holdings of nearly 3.4 million volumes and 5.3 million microforms, and maintained subscriptions to almost 19,000 paid serials. The total number of separately managed electronic journals was slightly more than 7,500; by 2004–2005, this number had increased to 8,600. As of September 2006, UB's Serials Solutions data summary indicated total electronic journal holdings of 60,380, including paid subscriptions, open access titles, and periodicals in full-text article databases. Of these e-journal holdings, 40,790 are indicated as unique. In 2003–2004, 38 percent of the libraries' total acquisitions budget was spent on electronic resources; the balance of expenditures has continued to move quickly in the digital direction since then, and by the end of 2004–2005, 59 percent of the libraries' budget was being spent on electronic materials.

In June 2006, the university libraries migrated from NOTIS to Aleph, the integrated library system developed by Ex Libris. UB's online catalog, known as BISON, is fundamental to library services, and in addition to bibliographic records for traditional library materials, it includes records and links for most electronic resources, with the exception of periodicals in article databases. The libraries use OCLC as their bibliographic utility. CTS is a longstanding member of BIBCO and NACO; HSL and more recently, CTS, are associate-level members of the Cooperative Online Serials Program (CONSER).

Since the mid-1990s, the collection of electronic resources, which initially was comprised primarily of abstracting and indexing (A&I) databases and journals that offered free access as a byproduct of paid print subscriptions, has grown steadily through the acquisition of individual titles as well as through a number of consortial arrangements for electronic journal packages. UB is an affiliate member of the NorthEast Research Libraries consortium, and a full member of the Western New York Library Resources Council, the State University of New York's SUNYConnect initiative (which shares electronic collections and services among the sixty-four campuses), and Nylink (the regional OCLC network and broker for electronic databases). It is also the largest member of the Library Consortium of Health Institutions in Buffalo, which maintains the Hospital and University at Buffalo Library Resource Network (HUBNET), and is a participant in the Westchester Academic Library Directors Organization (WALDO), a membership organization that supports the procurement and administration of electronic resources.

From the mid-1990s, when electronic resources arrived on the scene, through the end of 2004, electronic resources were independently acquired and managed by the technical services departments in CTS, HSL, and the law library. Efforts were made to standardize the bibliographic control of electronic resources, including a decision to include separate electronic version records for each provider of an electronic journal in BISON; for example, if UB has access to a title directly from the publisher and through two aggregator databases, three records are added to the catalog. A highly acclaimed, detail-rich A–Z list was developed and maintained by the libraries, but as the number of electronic journals steadily increased, these informative records were regretfully given up and creation of a simple title-subject A–Z list was outsourced to Serials Solutions.[3] Despite attempts to standardize records and access, the three technical services areas worked at different rates of speed, interpreted some standards differently, and one even continued to expand independently developed title and subject e-journal lists for that unit's Web pages. As a result, a significant amount of duplicative work was done, often not in exactly the same way.

By 2000, several key library staff recognized that in order to manage the increasing collection of electronic resources, a shared electronic resource management database, such as MIT's VERA, was needed.[4] A database structure intended to track every conceivable aspect of the libraries' e-materials was meticulously developed but languished due to lack of dedicated staff to collect, input, and maintain data. While some aspects of electronic resource management were more or less on track and users were receiving reasonably good service, there was room for a great deal of improvement.

Creating an Improved Structure for Electronic Resources Management

In 2003–2004, HSL began the shift from print or print-plus-online to electronic-only subscriptions and 90 percent of its $1.25 million acquisitions budget was spent on periodicals, e-journals, and databases. At that time, two of four clerical staff members in HSL's collection management services (CMS) were involved in monograph collection development, acquisitions, and copy cataloging; because both staff members were on the verge of retirement, it seemed to make little sense to train them in the intricacies and vagaries of handling electronic resources. The two other staff members had their hands more than full with print periodical ordering, receiving, claiming, binding, union listing, and handling the library's invoice payments and bookkeeping. In addition, the senior of these two staff members also acquired and performed copy cataloging of materials for the media collection, oversaw database cleanup projects underway in advance of Aleph migration, and handled weeding and massive retrospective barcoding projects that were undertaken in preparation for moving pre-1985 journals to a storage facility. A half-time librarian assisted with selection and deselection activities and maintained a subject-specific A–Z e-journal list that was developed prior to the introduction of the Serials Solutions list. Because this e-journal list is subject-oriented and considered invaluable by the HSL's specialized clientele, it continues to be maintained. The head of CMS administered the department and the acquisitions budget; supervised and evaluated staff; managed journal selection and deselection (including annual cancellation projects); handled all aspects of e-journal management (researching prices, registering for access, negotiating licenses, and coordinating with CTS regarding licenses); cataloging periodicals and serials (including CONSER work); selected monographs in specific subject areas; and served on a number of committees and task forces, including both the storage facility task force and a SUNY-wide collections committee involved in a multiyear renegotiation of a major big deal. A librarian in charge of monograph collection development and a half-time cataloger who split time between HSL and CTS rounded out the staff of CMS.

In CTS, prior to 2001, one librarian, three professional staff, and one civil service staff member in the periodicals section of acquisitions absorbed most e-periodicals management tasks in addition to handling the usual array of activities involved in acquiring and binding many thousands of titles. Serial, print periodical, and original e-journal cataloging were done in the cataloging department; however, e-journal copy cataloging was done in the periodicals section. In 2001, a second librarian was hired to help with the growing e-journal cataloging workload and to handle license negotiation and management. Other technologically savvy staff in CTS originally activated UB's holdings in Serials Solutions and developed a routine to extract data from BISON to export information to Serials Solutions for titles not included in any of the aggregator packages or databases. Serials Solutions integrated UB's local data with the data it managed on behalf of the libraries and included both in the monthly A–Z list update. As previously indicated, the method for coding BISON data for the extraction routine was communicated to HSL and the law library as well as to CTS's periodicals section staff. The SFX link server used by the libraries was never part of the technical services workload, but was assigned to the office of Web development.

By spring 2004, electronic resource management had become a high-priority issue for technical services staff in both CTS and HSL. Five individuals from the two units began to discuss the state of electronic periodicals management in the university libraries and how to improve it. It was quickly recognized that because both units were acquiring fewer monographs, one way to improve the situation would be to shift staff from monograph acquisitions to work on electronic periodicals. While this would have alleviated the situation within CTS to some degree, it would not have helped the HSL situation due to the pending retirements and no firm administrative commitment to replacing these individuals. It was ultimately decided that centralizing e-journal management would be the best way to achieve the desired improvements. In fact, it made sense on many levels to centralize most technical services activities for the two units.

After considerable research, deliberation, and discussion, a reorganization plan emerged. Rather than develop a hybrid super-periodicals department to handle both print and electronic periodicals, a new unit devoted exclusively to the management of electronic periodicals, serials, and subscription databases was envisioned. This scenario would allow several staff to concentrate on e-journal activities without being distracted by the physical presence of printed issues. It would also develop deeper expertise in additional staff, so there would be solid backup when the librarians who usually handled electronic periodical problems were unavailable. Periodical subscriptions with print and online versions would be considered primarily electronic because surveys and usage statistics indicated that UB's users had a strong preference for electronic access.

Another factor in the plan to develop an electronic periodicals and database department was the nearly simultaneous decision made by the university libraries to purchase the Innovative Interfaces, Inc. (III) Electronic Resource Management (ERM) system. The new department would also be responsible for developing, implementing, and maintaining that increasingly critical service. The final reorganization plan created both a print periodicals and serials section (PPSS) and an electronic periodicals management department (EPMD) within CTS. Preliminary plans for the reorganization were announced in both CTS and HSL in August 2004. The target date for implementing the reorganization was January 2, 2005. EPMD would be staffed by five of the six staff members who had formerly worked in the periodicals section, while the sixth moved to PPSS, as did a staff member from the section that handled monograph ordering, receiving, and copy cataloging (figure 1).

Two equal co-heads, the former head of the periodicals section and the head of HSL's CMS, would administer the new department. Other CMS staff remained at HSL. The two CMS staff members who were on the verge of retiring did so in 2005. One remaining CMS clerical staff member continued to handle HSL's print periodical check-in, claiming and binding, while the senior staffer handled union listing, assisted the new head of CMS (the former head of monograph selection) with collections-related activities, and absorbed some support activities for the HSL director's office. The half-time librarian continued to upgrade and maintain HSL's A–Z list and began to assist the new head of CMS with journal selection and deselection projects. The cataloger who was already split between CMS and CTS continued to work in both units, but spent more time in CTS (figure 2).[5]

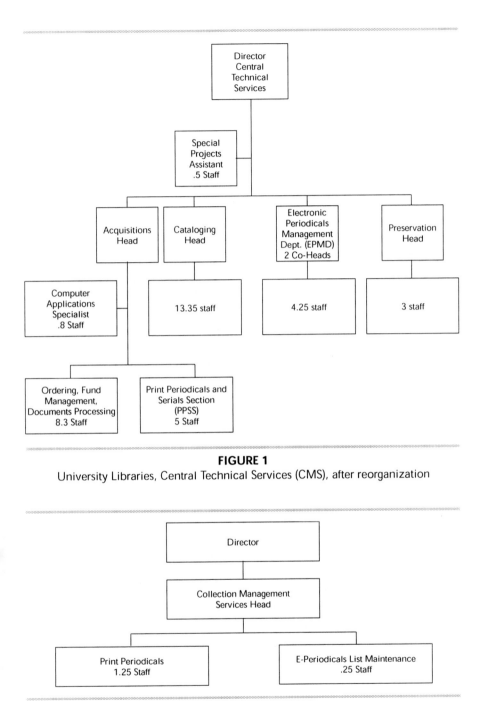

FIGURE 1
University Libraries, Central Technical Services (CMS), after reorganization

FIGURE 2
HSL's Collection Management Services (CMS), after reorganization

Implementation Issues and Strategies

EPMD was launched in January 2005 with three librarians, three professional staff, and a quarter-time cataloger borrowed from the cataloging department. All six full-time members of the department had previous experience with print periodicals and their experience with e-serials management ranged from a little to a great deal. The department was charged with the acquisition and timely, accurate management of electronic periodicals for all units within the university libraries except the law library. In addition, it took on implementation and ongoing management of III ERM and the acquisition and management of subscription-based databases (databases and electronic monographs were to be cataloged in the cataloging department). Workflows were devised or revised to increase accuracy and efficiency; departmental strategies and successes were communicated to the staff of the university libraries. Opportunities to collaborate with and provide leadership to other libraries within the SUNY system were explored, and within several months EPMD began to track the titles in SUNY's ScienceDirect Freedom Collection for the sixty-four campuses. EPMD staff members were urged to keep abreast of evolving trends, tools, and standards through extensive reading and active involvement in relevant associations.

The main functions of EPMD were elaborated as follows:

- Electronic periodical and database acquisition and renewal
- License negotiation and management
- Bibliographic control of electronic periodicals
- Maintenance of holdings and URLs for the periodicals (through BISON and Serials Solutions)
- Development, implementation, and management of the ERM system
- Troubleshooting problem reports

Dividing responsibility for these tasks among the staff was the vital first step. It was also essential that everyone understand the role of the department co-heads. One, the former head of CMS at HSL, although not a trained cataloger, had CONSER experience, was conversant with cataloging issues, and was the logical choice to assume primary responsibility for bibliographic control of the electronic periodicals. She shared responsibility for original cataloging of e-periodicals and serials—which was divided along broad subject lines—with the quarter-time cataloger, who was an experienced monograph and electronic resources cataloger. He, in turn, was also available for consultation about difficult titles and general cataloging practices and policies. The second co-head had a thorough knowledge of e-journal and database acquisitions in CTS, and therefore, continued to handle the tasks related to acquisitions. The third full-time librarian in the new unit assumed responsibility for licensing issues, an activity that previously had been a shared responsibility. Other decisions about division of labor then took place. Each professional staff member was assigned to work with a portion of the alphabet because it was thought that ownership of a section of electronic titles would be helpful in building expertise and would allow each individual to work with every publisher, vendor, and platform. There was more than enough work involved in setting up new titles, dealing with problems, reviewing and updating holdings, keeping URLs current, and activating individual titles in Serials Solutions to keep a staff of six extremely busy.

Training was one of the biggest challenges the new managers faced. There was no time to develop elaborate training materials or even a well thought-out training schedule prior to the birth of the new department on January 2, 2005. Training had to be immediately developed in order for everyone to become productive. Each electronic periodical publisher, online provider, and subscription agent had so many unique characteristics that it proved to be nearly impossible to develop a one-size-fits-all set of procedures. Moreover, none of the staff was very familiar with Serials Solutions. Each project required a special set of written instructions that were subject to constant modifications as irregularities were uncovered. Bibliographic work is fairly standardized, even though cataloging rules and interpretations continue to evolve. One local decision, deriving multiple records in the online catalog from the aggregator-neutral OCLC record when UB has access to a single journal through more than one source, was a challenge that was immediately documented. Overall, cataloging issues proved to be less difficult for the staff than learning how to deal with questions about ever-changing access points. For example, staff had to understand the possibility that a title could move from one publisher or one platform to another without prior notice, and that they would have to put on their detective hats to figure out why a periodical previously found on publisher X's Web site suddenly turned up on publisher Y's platform. They also had to recognize that some publishers and aggregators put all volumes of a journal under the latest (or earliest) title, thus making it impossible to relate UB's holdings to OCLC records until additional bibliographic work was done. Finally, staff encountered a number of errors in numbering, missing issues and volumes, and other anomalies that required contact with the publisher or aggregator in question to report and correct the error. Each of these situations exposed the staff to the ever-changing, idiosyncratic, and not always logical world of electronic information and provided valuable experience for the many challenges to come.

The III ERM System

While the III ERM system was complex, it was viewed as more scalable than the homegrown ERM database that had been in use. Funding to maintain a UB-dedicated server at III's home office in Emeryville, California, was allocated, and the contract for the III ERM system was signed in August 2004. Seeing a return on this investment—after the significantly more detailed, locally developed ERM system never got off the ground—was a high priority for the university libraries. While plans for the reorganization of CTS and CMS were still being discussed, implementation of the III ERM began. In October 2004, the three full-time librarians in EPMD and the libraries' electronic resources coordinator went to III headquarters for training. After returning from the training session, these four and a staff member from the office of Web development began to develop the record structure for the ERM system. Once the desired structure was established and documented in a data dictionary, meetings were held with stakeholders from other areas of the libraries, including interlibrary loan, reference, and collection development, to review the record structure and proposed operation of the ERM system. Rather than train a large number of additional staff to search the ERM system or produce their own reports, the implementation team recommended that the report writer feature be used to generate relevant reports for the stakeholders. This recommendation was made for the following three reasons:

> The ERM system purchased by the university included only eight ports. Because at any given time as many as five EPMD staff might be entering and maintaining data and one port would be used whenever reports were being created, only two ports would be consistently available for three interlibrary loan units, several reference desks, and a large number of collection development staff.
>
> The III ERM client must be loaded on each workstation that will access the system. While that in itself is not a problem, the connection to the libraries' server at III can take a couple of minutes to be

established, during which time no other work can be done on the terminal. If the connection is left open in order to facilitate access, one of the ports is constantly engaged.

UB purchased only the backend, but not the public module, of the ERM system. The technical side of the ERM is fairly complicated. For public services staff already faced with learning and remembering how to search a vast number of databases with highly varying interfaces, this would have been one more database to master. Even if staff became comfortable with navigating the backend, because much of the information entered into the ERM system used codes or abbreviations, the occasional user would find it difficult to interpret the data.

With the approval of the various stakeholders, EPMD staff began to enter data into the ERM system in the late spring 2005. Discussions about workflow were critical to establishing a workable procedure. EPMD professional staff started to create resource records for each database, e-journal package, and individual e-journal subscription, and corresponding licensing information was subsequently created and attached to each record. The department head with the responsibility for acquisitions concentrated on the administrative aspects of the system, such as creating underlying templates and inputting values for drop-down choices. The staff member from the office of Web development assumed responsibility for creating and posting a series of locally developed reports each month and for generating other reports on demand.

Additional Challenges and Solutions

Not surprisingly, numerous challenges continued to arise as EPMD staff gained experience. In addition to establishing bibliographic control, maintaining holdings and URLS, and working on ERM records, the professional staff in the department also assumed responsibility for activating titles in and managing holdings data for subscribed periodicals in UB's Serials Solutions database. EPMD staff worked with the Serials Solutions data in the following ways:

- an entire package was activated and the holdings provided by the package's publisher or vendor were accepted as representing UB's holdings;
- specific titles in a package were activated and the holdings were accepted; or

- either an entire package was activated or specific titles within the package were activated, but all holdings had to be verified and many had to be customized.

When UB first began to use Serials Solutions, many of the libraries' individual journal subscriptions were not represented in aggregations or packages. Therefore, the head of acquisitions and the director of CTS developed a procedure to export BISON data for those individual journals to Serials Solutions. In turn, Serials Solutions processed that data along with the titles and holdings they provided to UB as a result of the activation of packages and aggregations; the exported data was processed and returned to UB as SUNY Buffalo Individual Holdings. The procedure for extracting data each month from BISON to send to Serials Solutions had been in place for a few years prior to the establishment of EPMD and depended on specific coding in lx of the 856 of these titles. The CTS staff, including periodicals, as well as staff in technical services at HSL and the law library, had received instruction on this procedure. However, as has been previously indicated, the instructions were not clearly or uniformly understood, and as a result, many titles were not properly coded and therefore were not represented in the A–Z list. Starting in January 2005, determining which titles needed to be added or corrected and exactly how to fix them fell to staff in EPMD. The co-heads of EPMD found training the staff so challenging that Serials Solutions was invited to provide a Web training session for everyone in the department. After receiving the additional training, and with new insight, EPMD staff began to view Serials Solutions as a true asset; they also began to activate specific titles in packages and aggregations that had formerly been handled by the BISON extraction and export routine.

Given the volatile nature of the electronic environment, EPMD staff knew that titles, URLs, and holdings associated with each electronic journal record in the catalog—as well as whether the full text could actually be retrieved—had to be monitored. A proactive approach was used to discover and correct problems; however, with many thousands of titles to review, it was necessary to find a way to automate some of the work in order to relieve staff from the tedious task of calling up every title manually. A "y" in the 856 lx was used to generate a report that included the URL link. Staff members were able to download the report to their computers rather than work with a printed copy of the report. A locally developed program helped them move through the list with only a few keystrokes: a click to open the URL, possibly another click to verify holdings, a click or two to verify access at the article level, and if no corrections were needed, a keyboard return to move to the next title in the list. The design of the report and customized programming made it possible to quickly move through long lists of titles where back volumes were likely to be added or other holdings information was likely to change.

The first project that the department undertook in January 2005 was the addition of several hundred new titles in SUNY's ScienceDirect Freedom Plan, titles activated by Elsevier that month. It was anticipated that the work would be relatively straightforward and that staff would be able to locate and download appropriate OCLC e-version records, then edit the records in BISON, and add local holdings information. However, Science-Direct did not recognize certain title changes, there were volume and issue numbering problems, and the beginning dates in Serials Solutions did not always correspond with beginning dates specified in SUNY's contract with Elsevier. Each subsequent database that was tackled uncovered new wrinkles and oddities. Instructions developed for one publisher had to be modified for another. Everyone in EPMD had contact with the customer service staff at the libraries' subscription agencies, publishers, and aggregators to work out problems. In the end, many anomalies were settled, but it was crystal clear that certain types of problems, such as lack of recognition of title changes, or title changes taking place with an incorrect issue, would never be resolved with some providers. For example, staff learned that one well-known aggregator bases the timing of title changes on when the printed issue included the new ISSN; therefore, the aggregator declares that publishers—not the Library of Congress—have correct information about the timing of title changes. As a result of the intransigence of the aggregator, some of its e-journal archives make no sense whatsoever.

Assessment and Plans for the Future

The reorganization of CMS and CTS had significant ramifications not only for the staff of CTS but also for HSL, where the staff experienced a profound sense of grief when most of the technical services functions that had been independently handled, cherished, and relied on for more than one hundred years were transferred to another unit within the university libraries. In fact, it was difficult for some staff throughout the libraries to comprehend why centralizing management of electronic periodicals and databases and merging services was necessary or even desirable. Despite the initial concerns regarding the reorganization, after a couple of months staff in CTS, HSL, and the university libraries in general came to understand the reasons behind the reorganization and to see that change could work for the better. For example, catalogers in CTS were trained to use NLM classification and subject headings, so that HSL materials were purchased and cataloged at least as quickly, and often more expeditiously, than prior to the reorganization. HSL still receives and binds its remaining print periodicals, but the tasks of ordering, claiming, and creating publication patterns to expedite serials checking are handled in CTS. Print periodicals management for the units served by CTS changed hands without losing a beat.

While there is room for additional improvements, EPMD has improved the overall management of electronic resources within the UB libraries. The accuracy of the Serials Solutions list has increased, more OCLC e-version records are being authenticated, new titles and title changes are being added to BISON sooner, problems are being resolved more quickly, and the ERM system is being populated with data. Initially EPMD staff members were anxious about the new organizational structure, the amount of learning involved, and the high expectations of library administration. At the same time, staff felt a sense of pride and autonomy in being associated and trusted with the creation of a cutting-edge department. Because everyone in EPMD shares a common service orientation and a willingness to learn, a solid team bond has been formed. The team is still learning how to achieve the goals that have been set and continues to articulate new goals, but everyone in the department faces the challenges with maturity and perspective.

The following specific plans laid out for EPMD's second year were realized earlier than anticipated:

- EPMD staff participated fully in the migration from NOTIS to Aleph; they readily became acquainted with e-periodical records and were comfortable working in the new system within a matter of days, although there are many thousands of records that remain to be reviewed and edited;

- EPMD staff are using Serials Solutions with greater understanding than in the first year; as a result, better information is being provided to patrons and staff in the A–Z list;

  a CONSER Serials Cataloging Cooperative Training Program (SCCTP) trainer provided EPMD, cataloging, and interested acquisitions staff in CTS and at the law library with two days of basic serials and e-serials training; now the records everyone works with daily are better understood and can be better maintained through the CONSER program;

  the ERM system has been populated with data about all of the libraries' currently subscribed databases and e-journal packages, and work is underway to add resource, license, and contact records for the thousands of individual e-journals to which the libraries subscribe; and

- staff members have promoted EPMD through written reports in the community and library literature and through presentations at meetings and conferences.

The following goals have yet to be fully realized:

- consistent internal documentation for procedures and policies and a departmental presence on the CTS Web site; and
- solicitation of regular feedback from the libraries' staff and users about the access that EPMD provides to electronic resources. It would be helpful to find out what EPMD is doing right, where the department can still make improvements, and what is not being done that needs to be tackled.

What Should a Technical Services or Library Manager Do?

While centralizing most technical services, developing a new department to handle a significant portion of electronic resources, and shifting staff from one library or section to another worked for UB, the same scenario may not work equally well in other institutions. In fact, no one at UB expects technical services to remain configured as it currently is for long. Change is a fact of life in CTS, and the staff believes that the unit will continue to evolve as the information environment and the needs and expectations of users change.

So what should a technical services or library manager interested in improving the management of electronic resources do? The advice offered here does not focus on change management processes—there is a sizeable amount of literature available on the topic that can be consulted. Instead, the authors explain that if new staff cannot be added to deal with new workloads, managers must be creative and make difficult decisions about re-engineering the existing organization to handle pressing new demands. Asking staff to absorb additional work managing e-resources without changing other duties might mean that these highly capable individuals will not be able to keep up with the volume of work or cope with the amazing complexity of the tasks. Along with considering outsourcing options to publication access management services (PAMS), such as Serials Solutions or TDNet, and subscription agencies, reorganization and retraining may be the only realistic alternatives for effectively managing electronic resources. Although redescribing or renaming existing positions using such terms as *electronic resource librarian, electronic resources serials librarian, electronic resources cataloger, license specialist,* or *metadata specialist* may help set a new direction, this alone is not sufficient to solve the workload problems that occur. Retraining and ongoing retooling are also necessary and must be factored into whatever changes are recommended. There is no rule of thumb for the number or type of staff a library needs to cope with the massive workload associated with electronic resources.

When reviewing workloads and organizational structures, library managers and administrators should consider both the big picture and the finer details. Incentives and rewards as well as training and support should ease staff concerns associated with relearning, retooling, and moving into a new and unfamiliar work situation. Managers should make a sincere effort to review the capabilities and interests of the staff in a fair and unbiased fashion. Staff should be retrained to deal with complex tasks and myriad details surrounding electronic resources. Everyone should be given an opportunity to enhance his or her skills and encouraged to offer creative ideas for improving the daily work. Human resources managers should offer insight into how to introduce, promote, and manage change and alleviate the inevitable anxieties that arise. Extensive brainstorming sessions or a retreat with staff could help to provide an opportunity to explore ideas for coping and answer such questions as the following:

> Are the library staff members in touch with users, and do they know what kinds of resources those users need now as well as what type of resources they will require in both the near and long term?
>
> Where are the library's purchasing trends headed?
>
> Are print subscriptions being dropped in favor of e-journals?
>
> Is the library binding fewer volumes than it did in the past?
>
> Are fewer printed books being bought and cataloged?
>
> Is there a noticeable drop in circulation of materials?
>
> Does the library include or plan to include access to e-resources in its online catalog or through an A–Z list or a series of subject lists on its Web site?
>
> Does the library want to provide access to free electronic resources (for example, open access journals and government information) as well as to the materials for which it pays?
>
> To what extent is the library willing or able to incorporate PAMS and subscription agencies into the e-access picture?
>
> To how many consortia does the library belong, and to how many more resources will the library provide access as a result of those arrangements?

Does the number and complexity of the electronic resources being acquired require the implementation of an ERM system?

Has the library implemented or does it intend to implement a linking service, such as SFX, and, if so, who will be responsible for the creation and maintenance of the knowledge base that is required?

Does the library or institution have a proxy server that enables off-site users to access online materials?

Who resolves reports of abuse of e-resources received from publishers and aggregators?

Is there someone on the library staff with responsibility for reviewing and signing license agreements, or must all agreements be reviewed and signed by university legal counsel or purchasing departments?

How much information about licenses do the staff and users need to know?

Is the library considering any aspect of preservation scanning or participation in an archiving service, such as Lots of Copies Keeps Stuff Safe (LOCKSS) or Portico?[6]

Is the library involved in or might it become involved in implementing and maintaining an institutional repository?

By providing answers to these and similar questions, a vision for the future of the library's collections and services should emerge. While resistance to the vision is likely, both staff and users need to be encouraged to embrace it, along with relevant priorities and goals. If one of the institution's articulated priorities is to create an increasingly digital collection, staff at all levels need to understand the reason for the decision.

Although it is a very time-consuming process, by developing a plan and then adhering to it, an organizational strategy that meets the needs of the institution within the framework of available resources will be formed. Some institutions will find it sufficient to designate one or two staff members to handle the majority of the ERM workload. Others will give many or even most staff a role in electronic resource acquisition and management. Some institutions will create new departments or specialized groups within existing departments with responsibility for the burgeoning workload, while others may even elect to share the work of purchasing and managing electronic resources with sister institutions. The options are numerous and varied. Managers should be flexible and responsive in order to adapt to ongoing change, while at the same time being mindful that whatever solution is arrived at is likely to continue to evolve over time. If those working in a modern academic library have not already realized that change is constant, they need to become accustomed to that fact. CTS at UB long ago embraced change. Periodic changes in the structure of CTS and constant training and retraining of staff have allowed the UB libraries to effectively manage e-resources for the benefit of users and give the staff pride in knowing they are doing the best they can to fulfill the libraries' service mission.

REFERENCE NOTES

1. Martha Kryillidou and Mark Young, "ARL Library Trends," ARL Statistics & Measurement Program, 2003–2004" (Association of Research Libraries, Washington, D.C. 2004), www.arl.org/stats/arlstat/04pub/04intro.html (accessed 15 September 2006).

2. There are three categories of staff in the libraries: faculty librarians, professional, and classified (civil service). Faculty librarians, referred to as librarians in this paper, are tenure-track and hold academic rank. There are six levels of professional positions: only those at grade 4 and higher may require an MLS or other advanced degree. However, there are many MLS holders in grade 3 positions, and even some in grade 2. Librarians achieve tenure and professionals may achieve permanent appointment, which is primarily based on job performance after six years of service. Classified staff members are covered by New York State Civil Service rules. The UB staffing configuration is not necessarily representative of other SUNY institutions.

3. George S. Machovec, "Electronic Journal Market Overview," Serials Review 23, no. 2 (Summer 1997): 31–44. In Machovec's article, the UB e-journal list was hailed as "among the best of the noncommercial electronic journal web sites."

4. Ellen Finnie Duranceau, "License Tracking," Serials Review 26, no. 3 (October 2000): 69–73.

5. Organization charts of CTS and CMS provide a visual representation of how the two staffs were structured to handle electronic and print periodical workloads as of 1 January 2005.

6. For information about LOCKSS, see www.lockss.org/lockss/Home; for information about Portico, see www.portico.org/ (accessed 15 September 2006).

Science and Engineering Serials: Issues and Challenges in the Electronic Environment

ROBERT C. MICHAELSON, ANNA WU REN,
AND DANA L. ROTH

Science and engineering journals have long presaged trends in scholarly communication as a whole. Together with medical journals, these journals have always been the most expensive titles as well as those that increased most rapidly in price. Thus they were at the forefront of a shift in library purchasing away from monographs toward collections that are heavily comprised of serials. Science and engineering journals were also among the first to adopt online versions and to provide links to citations and other enhancements, such as rotatable images and multimedia. In additon, the science, technology, and medicine (STM) community was the first to introduce early open access (OA) models, such as arXiv.

Pricing Issues: The Core Problem

Based on past trends among all scholarly journals, including STM journals, the most important consideration concerns price. However, the business model used by many commercial STM publishers, in which researchers provide articles and refereeing services to publishers for free, who in turn sell them back to the researchers' institutions at a substantial premium, is quickly becoming unsustainable as a result of the following factors:

Over a ten-year period, subscription prices have increased an average of 7 percent per annum, resulting in a doubling of prices.

Often European-based STM publishers have not adjusted prices in accordance with fluctuating foreign exchange rates but rather have taken advantage of currency fluctuations, which has been especially harmful for dollar-based customers.

Many established journals, particularly those that are part of large package purchases, have chronically low ISI impact factors. There are significant differences in cost-effectiveness (where cost-effectiveness is the inverse of Barschall's measure of cost per 1000 characters/ impact factor when compared with nonprofit and society journals).[1] Some long-established publications with low-impact factors publish so many articles that canceling them is difficult—a problem exacerbated by packages of journals with limitations on cancellation—despite their poor cost-effectiveness.

Increased dependence on big deals, in which libraries acquire electronic access to a publisher's entire list for a price based on a combination of factors. Some big deals preclude cancellations, forcing libraries to retain every title offered, including those with low-impact factors or those that might be peripheral or marginal to the library's mission.

Academically sound, inexpensive OA titles published by nonprofit organizations and scholarly societies are offered as an alternative to high-priced commercial publications.

As a result, a serious disconnect exists between the cost per article, cost per page, and cost-effectiveness of commercially published journals versus those published by learned societies. Although individual STM journals enjoy a quasi-monopoly, studies of journals in specific subjects or with specific content make it possible to compare costs.

Subscription Price Increases

Academic libraries have a long history of acceding to faculty requests when specific journal titles are desired. However, this approach to serials collection management is rapidly becoming untenable. Collection development policies should reflect more quantitative selection measures, namely quality, price and availability, and usage. While many faculty members are either unaware or unconcerned about the pricing of their favorite journals, an important aspect of a librarian's responsibilities is making the academic community aware of price increases. One mechanism to raise awareness is to compare costs for related titles and present users with the raw data in a number of ways.

Simple subscription cost comparisons quickly put the problem into perspective (table 1). Combining this data with pagination comparisons sharpens this perspective and gives faculty members solid data for decision making (tables 2 and 3).

TABLE 1
Cost Comparisons for Related Titles

JOURNAL	SUBSCRIPTION COST						TOTAL ($)
	2000	2001	2002	2003	2004	2005	
Inorganic Chemistry	1,782	1,889	2,021	2,208	2,418	2,604	$12,922
Dalton Transactions	2,295	2,363	2,363	2,475	2,698	2,965	$15,159
Polyhedron	5,146	5,492	5,849	6,288	6,697	7,049	$ 36,521
Inorganica Chimica Acta	6,302	6,726	7,163	7,701	8,202	8,633	$ 44,727

TABLE 2
Pagination Comparison for Related Titles

JOURNAL	NUMBER OF PAGES						TOTAL PAGES
	2000	2001	2002	2003	2004	2005	
Inorganic Chemistry	6,145	7,104	7,170	8,910	8,657	9,977	47,900
Dalton Transactions	4,701	3,671	4,754	4,780	4,208	3,928	26,042
Polyhedron	2,770	3,423	2,885	3,621	3,273	3,118	19,090
Inorganica Chimica Acta	4,148	3,427	4,148	5,064	4,644	4,588	26,019

TABLE 3
Cost-per-Page Comparisons for Related Titles

JOURNAL	COST PER PAGE ($)						TOTAL ($)
	2000	2001	2002	2003	2004	2005	
Inorganic Chemistry	0.29	0.27	0.28	0.25	0.28	0.26	0.27
Dalton Transactions	0.49	0.64	0.50	0.52	0.64	0.75	0.58
Polyhedron	1.86	1.60	2.03	1.74	2.05	2.26	1.91
Inorganica Chimica Acta	1.52	1.96	1.73	1.52	1.77	1.88	1.72

Fluctuations in the Foreign Exchange Rate

Following the introduction of floating exchange rates, the U.S. dollar (USD) increased against the Deutsch Mark (DM) from $0.31 at the end of 1972 to $0.41 by mid-1973. This alone led to a one-year 32 percent increase in USD subscription prices without any change in subscription rates. By early

1980, the exchange rate had leveled off at $0.59 DM, and then began to decline until it reached a low of $0.31 DM in March 1985. Although some commercial publishers appeared to take advantage of this situation and explained the need for higher subscription prices on inflation and increased scientific output, the rising value of the USD versus European currencies meant that USD prices remained fairly stable in the early 1980s.[2]

This relatively benign period for U.S. libraries presaged the serials crisis of 1985–88, in which the DM increased to $0.62 in 1988, resulting in skyrocketing USD subscription prices. For example, during this period *Cell and Tissue Research* posted a USD increase of 90 percent from $1,121 to $2,133, while the DM subscription rate increased only 18 percent.[3] Throughout the 1990s, exchange rates remained relatively stable, with the average cost of a DM peaking at $0.63 in 1997. Thereafter, the DM again began to decline against the USD, and U.S. libraries experienced very small (approximately 3 percent) subscription price increases in 1998 and (approximately 2 percent) decreases in 1999.

In 2000, the major European commercial publishers took a radically different approach to subscription pricing. They simply disassociated the USD subscription price from the DM—and subsequently, the euro—and no longer offered subscriptions to North American libraries at the converted euro price, thus guaranteeing annual price increases. Had previous pricing formulas been followed, U.S. libraries would have realized significant annual savings. Table 4 lists the actual USD subscription rates for 2000–2006, compared with the rates based on the pre-2000 pricing policy (in parentheses).

TABLE 4
Actual USD Pricing (USD Pricing under Pre-2000 Policy)

JOURNAL TITLE	2000	2001	2002	2003	2004	2005	2006
BBA*	11,362	12,127	12,915	13,884	14,786	15,599	16,418
	(10,895)	(9,535)	(10,504)	(11,120)	(13,852)	(16,595)	(18,640)
Brain Research	16,344	17,444	18,578	19,971	21,269	22,386	23,617
	(15,673)	(13,716)	(15,109)	(15,996)	(19,926)	(23,813)	(26,749)

*Biochimica et Biophysica Acta

ISI Impact Factors, Journal Quality, and Cost-Effectiveness

A journal's ISI impact factor is the ratio of a given year's citations to articles published during the previous two years.[4] For example, if X = the number of 2005 citations to articles published in 2003 and 2004, and Y= the number of articles published in 2003 and 2004, then Z= X/Y is the 2005 impact factor. ISI impact factors are widely accepted as the measure of a journal's quality. Comparisons of ISI impact factors are only valid within specific subjects and content formats. For example, a comparison of impact factors of inorganic chemistry journals is shown in table 5.

While there may be overall concerns about the validity of comparing impact factors, the general trend, as revealed by table 5, confirms the overall quality of *Inorganic Chemistry* (American Chemical Society) and *Dalton Transactions* (Royal Society of Chemistry) compared with *Polyhedron* (Pergamon/Elsevier) and *Inorganica Chimica Acta* (Elsevier). Impact factors are also useful in extending the cost-per-page data to measure cost-effectiveness as may be seen in table 6.[5]

At a minimum, these values indicate that *Inorganic Chemistry* is more cost-effective than its commercial counterparts by a factor of about 14. The data also suggest that for *Polyhedron* and *Inorganica Chimica Acta* to be as cost-effective as *Inorganic Chemistry*, their 2005 subscription prices would have to have been $418 and $492 respectively, rather than $7,049 and $8,633.

TABLE 5
Comparison of ISI Impact Factors for Selected Inorganic Chemisty

JOURNAL TITLE	2000	2001	2002	2003	2004	2005
Inorganic Chemistry	2.7	3.0	3.0	3.4	3.5	3.9
Dalton Transactions	2.5	2.8	3.0	2.9	2.9	3.0
Polyhedron	1.0	1.2	1.4	1.6	1.6	2.0
Inorganica Chimica Acta	1.2	1.4	1.6	1.6	1.6	1.6

TABLE 6
Comparison of Cost-Effectiveness Data for Selected Inorganic Chemistry Journals (Normalized Cost-per-Page/Impact Factor)

JOURNAL TITLE	2000	2001	2002	2003	2004	2005	AVERAGE
Inorganic Chemistry	1.00	1.00	1.00	1.00	1.00	1.00	1.00
Dalton Transactions	1.82	2.54	1.79	2.44	2.76	3.73	2.52
Polyhedron	17.38	14.81	15.59	14.80	16.02	16.87	15.91
Inorganica Chimica Acta	11.83	15.56	11.63	12.93	13.83	17.54	13.89

Three major commercial publishers currently offer deals based on previous print subscriptions (Elsevier's ScienceDirect, Springer-Link, and Wiley's Enhanced Access License). The arrangements differ and seem to be in constant flux and subject to negotiation. While there are some obvious benefits to these types of arrangements (especially if consortia arrangements are offered), either directly or indirectly, they inhibit libraries from carrying out their responsibilities for managing their collections by requiring either multiyear commitments or annual cost increases.

The concept of OA is based on the premise that research funded by public agencies and published in scholarly journals should be freely available.[6] Many scholars believe that OA may offer a solution to the budget problems facing libraries, and some library users and university administrators have even been led to believe that OA journals are available free of charge, making it difficult for libraries to make the case for increased funding.[7] Because OA publishers often receive financial support in the form of grants from foundations, and donations, sponsorships, and memberships from private citizens, universities, and profit or nonprofit organizations, they may compete with traditional journals for money that would in the past have been used to fund traditional subscriptions.

The misconception that access to OA journals is free creates difficulties for librarians, who must convince administrators that increased funding is needed not only to keep pace with serials price increases and but also to allow them to continue the transition from print to electronic collections. Journals offered on so-called OA Web sites are often based on per-article charges or membership fees that are ongoing, unpredictable, and almost always beyond the library's control, rather than based on traditional subscription fees. Because there are no standards of quality for OA journals, it remains to be seen whether they will be successful in the highly competitive world of scientific publishing. Before replacing traditional journals with OA titles, libraries should carefully consider the various OA models, contribution structures, and pricing arrangements offered:

> The OA-journal model requires authors or sponsors to pay a publication fee. Because journal article publication cannot be truly free, an obvious alternative to subscriptions (i.e. reader pays) is the assessment of author charges. Until recently page charges for publication had been a long-standing practice, particularly among society publishers, and this sharing of publication costs between authors and subscribers enabled societies to maintain reasonable subscrip-

tion rates. In the last few years, this practice has been largely abandoned because of intense competition from commercial publishers who do not assess any page charges.[8]

The author-pays model might be viewed as a major threat to commercial publishers because authors and sponsors would obviously favor lower-cost publishers with lower charges, and the competitive impact would be chiefly on commercially published journals that are overpriced by such metrics as cost-per-page/impact factor.

The self-archiving, or repository, model depends on the author to post an electronic version of the article. Often the article is not in its final state, but rather, is a preprint version that is very close to the final version. This model may be seen as a more modern version of the reprint card system that was used to obtain copies of articles before the advent of photocopy machines. As the volume of OA research available on the Web increases, its impact will likely have a disproportionate effect on commercial publishers because very high-priced titles are most likely to be dropped if libraries find that access to self-archived articles is an acceptable substitute for the journal itself. Commercial vendors are beginning to respond to these variant access models by, for example, allowing authors to post the final version of articles on a personal or institutional Web site.[9]

The embargo model seems to be preferred by nonprofit publishers, such as PubMed Central and the Royal Society of Chemistry, because it provides access to publications after varying periods of time. PDF versions of articles published between specific years are accessible, and a year's worth of content is added at the beginning of each new year.[10]

The hybrid model includes a wide variety of print and electronic combinations, incorporating features of the other models. For example, JBC Papers in Press provides access to articles accepted by the *Journal of Biological Chemistry* prior to copyediting and publication. Articles from the previous year become freely available on January 1 of the following year. JBC receives about one-third of its publication costs from page charges to authors ($75 per page, plus charges for tables and figures) and about two-thirds from subscription revenues, primarily from libraries.[11] In addition to providing free access to all nonarticle material, such as editorials, letters to the editor, book and software reviews, the International Union of Crystallography offers access to any current or previously published research article for a fee of $800.[12] Springer maintains a similar policy that provides a mix of both standard subscriber-only papers with OA papers for authors willing to pay a processing fee of $3,000 in addition to any charges for special processing, such as color or extra length.[13] EDP Sciences, co-publisher, with Springer, of the *European Physical Journal*, also publishes *EPJdirect*; originally both access and submission were free.[14]

Questions of Content, Archiving, and Access

Librarians have a long history of dealing with print journals—a perspective that continues to influence many of their decisions. For example, the libraries of the University of California system and Harvard University, as well as the Center for Research Libraries, are partnering with JSTOR to preserve print copies of all volumes in the JSTOR electronic archive.[15] Preserving print editions at multiple locations will insure long-term preservation of journal content using time-proven techniques. Questions about content are closely linked to matters of archiving. What must be archived? What, if anything, is the copy of record? What is the preferred or authoritative copy? Which version of an article is the one to which a patron should be referred, and to which version should a direct link be made from an online database? Unfortunately, traditional archiving techniques are no longer appropriate; the online versions of many journals contain material, such as extensive data, videos, and other multimedia, that does not exist in the print version. In fact, for an increasing number of journals, there is no such thing as a print version. Librarians must turn their attention to preservation of online content because the print version is rapidly becoming a lingering remnant of the past, like a buggy-whip holder on an early horseless carriage.

As electronic journals become ubiquitous, particularly in the sciences, engineering, and technology fields, the online versions of journals are often considered the versions of record (the versions deemed authoritative in case of a discrepancy). It is possible that there may be several online versions of a publication, so distinguishing among them is very important. Publishers frequently include additional features in the electronic version, such as full-text search capabilities, in an effort to make it the preferred version. Aggregators may provide digitized full-text versions of journals as well; however, these versions often lack internal links and illustrations or other critical components.[16]

Publishers may also limit the content of the online version. For example, the online edition of *Science* initially featured a section titled ScienceExpress, which gave individual members, but not institutional members, of the American Association for the Advancement of Science (AAAS) access to articles prior to publication. As the intricacies of online subscriptions are worked out, it is hoped that publishers will recognize the need to provide mechanisms to give both individual and institutional subscribers access to the entire content of their publications.

It is important to take note of the preprint archives that have become *de facto* primary sources of research articles in some fields. The pioneer in this arena is Paul Ginsparg's arXiv, which is considered the most important source of technical information for researchers in theoretical physics and mathematics.[17] The overwhelming acceptance of electronic preprints in many scientific disciplines means that publishers more readily allow authors to keep preprint versions, and in some cases, published versions of their papers on their personal Web sites after publication. An interesting study found that papers published in *Astrophysical Journal* and also posted on arXiv were cited more than twice as often as papers not posted there.[18] A comparison of citation rates for computer science papers that were freely available online with those not freely available electronically produced a similar finding.[19] While it is not possible to generalize across all disciplines based on these studies alone, the findings appear to make a persuasive case for the benefits of some form of OA.

Preservation of print is not the only task now facing libraries. Depending on the context, *archiving* may mean either the conversion of printed material into an electronic form or the procedures undertaken to ensure the preservation of content that is in electronic form. Converting print resources into electronic form now occurs almost routinely.[20]

Among researchers and librarians alike, one of the greatest causes of apprehension about the migration from a print to an electronic format is the complex matter of guaranteeing the integrity of the content. The scholarly community needs assurances that the complete content of journals will be reliably maintained and accessible in perpetuity. This requires, first of all, that the entire content of print journals be replicated in online versions, which is not always the case and, for security purposes, that the content is maintained at several independent sites and periodically and systematically refreshed. In addition, migration of the data must be possible as new formats and storage media are developed.

These concerns were exacerbated when the discovery was made that in an unknown number of journals, some print content had been excluded from the online versions. The online version of the June 2000 issue of

Mechanism and Machine Theory lacked the obituary of a distinguished engineer. In this instance, the decision to omit the material was made at the discretion of the editor. Due in large part to objections from librarians, a new policy was implemented so that "since approximately October 2001, the electronic capture rule is as follows: **"All items which appear in the table of contents of the physical printed issue will be captured electronically and made retrievable via ScienceDirect. Items which are not in the table of contents will not be available on ScienceDirect"** [bold face in original quote].[21] Incomplete archiving is not unique to commercial publications, and it would be desirable if publishers would commit to cover-to-cover archiving of their publications as is done for the journals archived in JSTOR or for the *Scientific American* Archive Online.

The inexorable decay of magnetic storage media and the anticipated changes in storage software and hardware create additional concerns about the stability of digitized material. Magnetic, optical, and electronic storage media degrade, distorting entire files. The possibility of human intervention to remove articles must also be considered.[22] An article in the *Chronicle of Higher Education* brought the matter to light and resulted in a revision to one publisher's policy on article withdrawal.[23] Under the terms of the new policy, retracted articles are retained in the database with an appropriate warning, unless legal ramifications are anticipated, in which case the text may be removed and a disclaimer added. Policies such as those announced by the American Physical Society are preferable:

> The American Physical Society has taken the position that articles, once put in place on line, should remain there as part of the scholarly record. We cannot, of course, guarantee that the appearance of a plagiarized article in one of our journals might not cause legal action on the part of another publisher to force us to remove the article. We would in that case try to negotiate with them to allow us to keep the article on line with a suitable acknowledgement that the article was plagiarized.[24]

In order to alleviate some of the concerns that have surfaced surrounding archiving and perpetual access, publishers are exploring a number of different strategies. In some instances, individual institutions have been allowed to maintain content on their own servers.[25] However, questions about the governing policies of such archives are still uncertain; for example, would the contributing publishers have authority over such matters as withdrawal of disputed publications? In other instances, publishers maintain their own mirror sites and ensure that in case their principal site should fail, a switch-over to an alternate site would seamlessly occur.

The Lots of Copies Keeps Stuff Safe (LOCKSS) project, initiated at Stanford University has taken a different approach to archiving by establishing a *dark* archive where electronic data is stored and can be accessed in the event of a problem with the publishers' servers.[26] Content from more than sixty publishers is maintained on a number of servers that automatically cross-compare content to assure stability. Currently only the documents themselves are loaded on the LOCKSS servers, not the links between documents or to other metadata, so the preservation is not complete, but LOCKSS is widely viewed as a useful starting point in the discussion about archiving.

Another approach to archiving, although it is one that is somewhat problematic, is author self-archiving. Because not all publishers allow this method of archiving and the process is dispersed rather than consolidated, coordinating the universe of publications is more difficult and lacks long-term assurance of accessibility.[27] Instead of a strategy for long-term archiving, perhaps self-archiving would be better viewed as an approach to OA. Unfortunately, a few publishers, notably the American Chemical Society (ACS), do not allow self-archiving or permit local loading of their journals. The society does not participate in LOCKSS, nor does it currently have a mirror site, and this lack of attention to archiving inhibits libraries from converting their ACS subscriptions to online only.

The rise in the availability of electronic journals has had a great impact on interlibrary loan (ILL) services. Standard practices commonly accepted in the print world are not universally recognized by providers of electronic publications; therefore, ILL provisions for electronic journals differ more than provisions for print and vary widely from publisher to publisher. Some publishers may allow electronic transmission of requested articles, while others permit only fax delivery. The most restrictive arrangements only permit copies from an electronic copy to be sent by mail to borrowing libraries.[28] Publishers that allow online purchase of individual articles may not permit ILL to for-profit entities. The interpretation of fair use in the print world is being challenged by some entities in the electronic realm. As a result, it is no longer possible to have a standard ILL process that applies to publishers, vendors, and aggregators. When negotiating license agreements, libraries should attempt to adhere to the fair-use principles recognized by both user communities and publishers in the print environment. While the formats are different, the current electronic environment should not change the concept of fair use.[29] As scientists often need information more quickly than researchers in other disciplines, they often seek other ways to secure articles, rather than deal with ILL procedures that may be hampered by complex license restrictions.

Conclusion

Nowhere have electronic journals been more enthusiastically embraced than in the STM community. Nonetheless, most libraries have experienced problems or been alerted to issues that are unique to an electronic environment. In order to complete the transition from a print to an electronic-only subscription arrangement, libraries need to convince their communities that electronic journals are at least as reliable and convenient as their print counterparts, if not more so. The reliability of electronic journal Web sites or servers and the timely uploading of new issues are important to the science and engineering communities where information must be shared and rapidly dispersed.

Publications in STM have traditionally been on the bleeding edge of serials issues, with the highest average costs, the biggest price increases, and the largest proportion of title changes and other cataloging challenges. Libraries, as early adopters of electronic journals, many with unique content, have learned to adapt to the challenges these resources present. STM publications have continued to present disproportionately large management challenges in the electronic milieu, including large numbers of publisher, URL, and aggregator changes, and the potential interruption in access resulting from these changes can be particularly disruptive in the rapidly moving STM fields. Because STM libraries adopted electronic journals (many with unique content) early on, they have learned to adapt to the challenges these resources present.

Although the management of electronic journals presents new problems, it also allows libraries to give up some traditional tasks, such as claiming undelivered issues, replacing defective issues, or grappling with incomplete volumes prior to binding. Many publishers have shown a willingness to learn from their customers; for example, by providing IP-based, site-wide access instead of the password-protected access that some publishers initially offered. Librarians are hopeful that publishers will continue to implement procedures that are beneficial to the scholarly community, and will work with, rather than in opposition to such scholars' initiatives as arXiv and the Public Library of Science, and adopt the best features of these experiments. As publishers, jobbers, aggregators, and libraries adapt to the electronic environment, it will be easier and less expensive for librarians to provide users with immediate access to important information.

REFERENCE NOTES

1. Henry H. Barschall, "The Cost of Physics Journals," *Physics Today* 39, no. 12 (December 1986): 34–36; Henry H. Barschall, "The Cost-Effectiveness of Physics

Journals," *Physics Today* 41, no. 7 (July 1988): 56–59; Henry H. Barschall and J. R. Arrington, "Cost of Physics Journals: A Survey," *Bulletin of the American Physical Society* 33, no. 7 (July-August 1988): 1437–47. For a compilation of journal value measures in many fields, see the University of Wisconsin's Journal Value Project at www.wendt.wisc.edu/projects/jvp/welcome.do (accessed 14 August 2006). See also Ted Bergstrom and Preston McAfee, Journal Cost-Effectiveness Web site, www.journalprices.com/ (accessed 14 August 2006).

2. Dana L. Roth, "Differential Pricing and Exchange Rate Profits," (Pasadena, Calif: California Institute of Technology Papers and Publications, 2002). http://resolver.caltech.edu/CaltechLIB:2002.008 (accessed 14 August 2006). Discussion of the differential pricing issue and its impact on librarians' attitudes toward some publishers.

3. Dana L. Roth, "The Serials Crisis Revisited," *Serials Librarian* 18, no. 1–2 (1990): 123–29.

4. For an explanation of the ISI impact factor, see "The Impact Factor," Thomson Scientific Web site, http://scientific.thomson.com/free/essays/journalcitationreports/impactfactor/ (accessed 12 August 2006).

5. Henry H. Barschall, "The Cost-Effectiveness of Physics Journals," *Physics Today* 41, no. 7 (July 1988): 56–59.

6. Charles W. Bailey, Jr., *Open Access Bibliography: Liberating Scholarly Literature with E-prints and Open Access Journals* (Washington, D.C.: Association of Research Libraries, 2005), www.escholarlypub.com/oab/oab.pdf (accessed 12 August 2006); *Serials Review* 30, no. 4 (2004); Directory of Open Access Journals Web site, www.doaj.org/ (accessed 14 August 2006). For potential budgetary benefits of OA, R. Stephen Berry "The Rationale for 'Full and Open Access' of Scientific Information," *The Transition from Paper: Where Are We Going and How Will We Get There?* ed. by R. Stephen Berry and Anne Simon Moffat (Cambridge, Mass.: AAAS, 2001), www.amacad.org/publications/trans15.aspx (accessed 14 August 2006).

7. David Goodman, "The Criteria for Open Access," *Serials Review* 30, no. 4 (2004): 258. One OA publisher describes its new publishing venture as "making the full contents freely available for anyone to read, distribute, or use for their own research." See the Public Library of Science Web site, www.plos.org/about/ (accessed 15 August 2006).

8. Examples of the OA journal model include Public Library of Science and BioMed Central, www.biomedcentral.com/ (accessed 15 August 2006); S. L. Rovner, "Opening Access: Publishers Weigh the Risks and Benefits of Free Online Journal Access," *Chemical & Engineering News* 83, no. 20 (2005): 40–44.

9. Examples of commercial publishers and scholarly societies that allow self-archiving include AIP, APS, IEEE, IOP, Wiley, and Springer. For comprehensive information on publisher's policies, see Eprints, "Journal Policies—List of Publishers," http://romeo.eprints.org/publishers.html (accessed 15 August 2006).

10. PubMed Central, www.pubmedcentral.nih.gov/ (accessed 15 August 2006).

11. JBC Online, www.jbc.org/pips/pips.0.shtml (accessed 15 August 2006).

12. International Union of Crystallography Submission to Science and Technology Committee of the House of Commons Inquiry into Scientific Publications, "Publishing Crystallography Journals in the Electronic Environment: The Experience of a Specialist Learned-Society Publisher," Evidence to the House of Commons Committee on Science and Technology Inquiry into Scientific Publications, U.K. (February 2004), www.iucr.org/iucr-top/iucr/stcttee04.html#open (accessed 15 August 2006).

13. Springer, "Springer Open Choice," www.springeronline.com/sgw/cda/frontpage/ 0,10735,1-40359-0-0-0,00.html (accessed 15 August 2006). Also see Peter Suber's comment on "Springer's Open Choice Program," Open Access News Blog, comment posted on 3 July 2004, www.earlham.edu/~peters/fos/2004_06_27_fosblogarchive .html#a108885692635508899 (accessed 15 August 2006).

14. Beginning in 2004, *EPJdirect* continued as online-only supplements in the *European Physical Journal, Sections A–E*. The EPJDirect Archive contains volumes 1–4 (1998–2003) of that free journal at www.edpsciences.org/journal/index.cfm?edpsname=epjdi rect&niv1=contents&niv2=archives (accessed 15 August 2006).

15. For details about the Center for Research Libraries project, see www.crl.edu/content. asp?l1=4&l2=19&l3=35&l4=62&l5=12 (accessed 15 August 2006).

16. For example, Wilson Select lacks links in the references for the Annual Review series.

17. arXiv, http://arxiv.org (accessed 14 August 2006). Preprints in the field of high-energy physics are also indexed by SPIRES at www.slac.stanford.edu/spires/hep/; computer science preprints are indexed at several servers, including Networked Computer Science Technical Reference Library at www.ncstrl.org/; mathematics preprint servers may be found at the Directory of Mathematics Preprint and E-print Servers at http://e-math.ams.org/global-preprints/; cognitive science and neuroscience has a site for self-archived preprints at Cogprints: Cognitive Sciences E-print Archive at http://cogprints.org/; E-print Network is a government Web site integrating scientific and technical e-prints from a wide range of sources at www.osti.gov/eprints/; another preprint metasite is Service Provider Web Site SAIL-eprints at http://eprints.bo.cnr. it/. Some libraries try to maintain listings of preprint servers, such as the University of Virginia Charles L. Brown Science and Engineering Library's Preprint Servers and Databases Web page at www.lib.virginia.edu/science/guides/s-preprn.htm and the John Crerar Library's Science Preprint and Open Access Servers Web page at www. lib.uchicago.edu/e/su/sci/preprints.html, but keeping the information up-to-date is very difficult. In general, successful preprint servers are associated with scholarly societies, universities, or other nonprofit entities; an attempt by Elsevier to create preprint servers in mathematics, chemistry, and computer science did not generate contributions "in sufficient numbers to justify further development" and new submissions were terminated on 24 May 2004. See the ScienceDirect Preprint Archive at www.sciencedirect.com/preprintarchive (accessed 15 August 2006). Some other servers that harvest Open Archives Initiative (OAI)–compatible preprint and other full-text sources are listed in Gerry McKiernan, "OAI Service Providers," *Science & Technology Libraries* 23, no. 1 (2002): 87–98, www.public.iastate.edu/~gerrymck/ OAISP.pdf (accessed 15 August 2006).

18. Greg J. Schwarz and Robert C. Kennicutt, Jr., "Demographic and Citation Trends in Astrophysical Journal Papers and Preprints," Cornell University Library arXiv.org, 10 November 2004, http://arxiv.org/PS_cache/astro-ph/pdf/0411/0411275.pdf (accessed 14 August 2006).

19. Steve Lawrence, "Online or Invisible?" Ivyspring International Publisher site, http://ivyspring.com/steveLawrence/SteveLawrence.htm (accessed 15 August 2006). Edited version appears as "Free Online Availability Substantially Increases a Paper's Impact," *Nature* 411, no. 6837 (31 May 2001): 521.

20. There are several examples, of which one of the earliest and most comprehensive is JSTOR (www.jstor.org), a subscription-based archive that was established through a grant from the Andrew W. Mellon Foundation. In addition to JSTOR, there are also

numerous efforts to create online archives of content for publications that had existed only in print such as the Bibliothèque nationale de France's Gallica (http://gallica .bnf.fr/periodiques.htm), the Numérisation de Documents Anciens Mathématiques/ Digitization of Ancient Mathematics Documents (www.numdam.org/en/); the Electronic Mathematical Archiving Network Initiative (www.emani.org/); the Japan Science and Technology Information Aggregator, Electronic (www.jstage.jst.go.jp/ browse/_journallist/-char/en); the Cornell University Albert R. Mann Library's Core Historical Literature of Agriculture (http://chla.mannlib.cornell.edu/c/chla/browse/ journals.html); to create online archives of content that had existed only in print; and some individual journals, such as the *American Journal of Science*, available www .geology.yale.edu/~ajs/Regular.html. Apart from JSTOR, all of these provide free access worldwide. A number of scientific societies, including the American Physical Society, American Physiological Society, the Institute of Physics, the American Chemical Society, the Royal Society of Chemistry, and the Society for Industrial and Applied Mathematics have digitized their publications and commercial publishers are doing the same. Some societies, such as the Korean Chemical Society (http://journal. kcsnet.or.kr/) have made their content available on the Web for free. Others provide free content up to a "moving wall;" for example, the *Proceedings of the National Academy of Sciences* (http://pnas.org) is available from volume 1 (1915) up to six months prior to the present date. (All accessed 15 August 2006.)

21. ScienceDirect Info, "Frequently Asked Questions," www.info.sciencedirect.com/ implementing/faq/ (accessed 15 August 2006). This is certainly an enormous improvement, and it is gratifying when a major publisher heeds customers, although a response (April 2005) by Elsevier to a complaint about missing content elicited the following comment: "currently have around 0.5% of missing content on ScienceDirect which is a significant reduction on the figures two years ago." However, there are still difficulties with the online content from both commercial and other publishers, and Elsevier has not indicated that it plans to rectify past omissions (the obituary, for example, is still not included in the online *Mechanism and Machine Theory*); the rule applies only to journals "published as part of Elsevier's core primary publishing program" and may not apply to journals in Elsevier affiliates, such as Cell Press. Some material, such as advertising, is seldom found in tables of contents, and thus will seldom be available online despite its value to researchers and historians.

22. The discussion concerned Elsevier policies that led to the expunging of more than thirty articles from ScienceDirect; they were withdrawn for various reasons, but in each instance the only information available on ScienceDirect was the notice "for legal reasons this article has been removed by the publisher."

23. Andrea Foster, *Chronicle of Higher Education* 49, no. 18 (10 January 2003): A27. For information on the Elsevier policy, see "Elsevier Policy on Article Withdrawal," www.info.sciencedirect.com/licensing/policies/withdrawal (accessed 15 August 2006).

24. Statement by Martin Blume, editor-in-chief of the American Physical Society, may be found at http://listserv.nd.edu/cgi-bin/wa?A2=ind0301&L=pamnet&P=R640 (accessed 15 August 2006).

25. Elsevier publications are *de facto* archived at OhioLINK, the University of Toronto Library, the British Library, Los Alamos National Laboratory, and other repositories, and they have a formal archiving agreement with Koninklijke Bibliotheek (Netherlands).

26. LOCKSS (http://lockss.stanford.edu/). A related preservation program, CLOCKSS (www.lockss.org/clockss/Home) has recently been launched to address global issues "in the event of a long-term business operation, or in making orphaned or abandoned works readily available to the scholarly community." (All accessed 14 August 2006.)

27. While the American Physical Society, American Institute of Physics, Royal Society of Chemistry, and recently, Elsevier, do currently allow self-archiving, the American Chemical Society does not. A very useful list of publishers' policies on self-archiving may be found at SHERPA, www.sherpa.ac.uk/romeo.php (accessed 14 August 2006).

28. Although *borrowing* libraries traditionally report statistics to the Copyright Clearance Center, some publishers require *lending* libraries to provide usage reports, putting an even greater burden on lending libraries.

29. American Society for Engineering Education Engineering Libraries Division, "Biennial Punch List of Best Practices for Electronic Resources," revised May 2005, http://eld .lib.ucdavis.edu/punchlist/PunchlistRevision2005.pdf (accessed 15 August 2006).

4

The Challenge of Serials Collection Evaluation in a Changing Environment: Examples from Northwestern University Library

HARRIET LIGHTMAN

With all aspects of serials management, delivery, and use dramatically changing, some of the traditional ways that librarians review journal collections—user surveys, circulation counts, citation analyses, reshelving studies, and consultations with relevant user groups—may be losing their validity.[1] Electronic delivery is changing the journal landscape so drastically that it is imperative for librarians not only to question the usefulness of some standard serials evaluation methods but also to develop new review techniques with criteria that can be adapted to fit the research behaviors of different academic disciplines, various types of libraries, and the evaluation skills of individual librarians.

Between 1998 and 2005, serials reviews for the economics, philosophy, and history collections at Northwestern University Library (NUL) were completed. The economics and philosophy reviews, which only included print titles, were relatively straightforward. The history serials review, on the other hand, focused on both print and electronic materials and was complicated to design and execute. Because there were no evaluation models in place that were specifically fitting for a hybrid collection, and because history titles were coming online as the review was taking place, the review methods grew and changed in the course of the study. Unanticipated questions also arose: Was the library paying for too many versions of particular titles, or subscribing to a print version when an electronic version would suffice, or both? Were old fiscal models still viable, given the plethora of formats, aggregated packages, freely available content, and vendor payment options? Is it even possible to review subject-specific jour-

53

nals comprehensively when the acquisition of aggregated packages changes the shape of a carefully developed subject collection and open access and freely available titles, while chiefly beneficial, may introduce less scholarly unselected materials to that collection?[2] The reasons why reviews of NUL's economics, philosophy, and history collections were initiated and the differences in the various evaluation methods highlights some of the ways in which collections of journals in academic libraries are changing, as well as the difficulties of tailoring a journal review to fit the research behaviors of a particular discipline.[3]

NUL Collections

NUL on the Evanston, Illinois, campus is comprised of the main library building and the Deering Library building, which are physically connected and house the general subject collections as well as a number of specialized departments and libraries: the Seeley G. Mudd Library for Science and Engineering, the Mathematics Library, and the Geology Library on the Evanston campus; and the Joseph Schaffner Library on the Chicago campus, which chiefly supports the School of Continuing Studies and the Managers' Program of the Kellogg School of Management. The NUL system also includes the Galter Health Sciences Library and the Pritzker Legal Research Center, both of which are located on the Chicago campus and are administratively separate from the other libraries. The libraries at Northwestern University hold more than 4.6 million volumes, 4.3 million microforms, and almost 42,000 current periodicals and serials. The collections discussed in this chapter are all part of the university library's main collection housed on the Evanston campus. Also on the Evanston campus, and an affiliate of NUL, is the United Library of the Garrett-Evangelical and Seabury-Western Theological Seminaries.

NUL has a complex collections budget and materials selection process. Each year, librarians with selection responsibilities receive an allocation of funds to purchase materials in support of a specific discipline or subject area; they also track expenditures for these disciplines/subject areas. Historically, the system has worked extremely well. In recent years, pricing models have become more complex, traditional subject boundaries have softened, and approval plans and large serials packages have absorbed greater sums of library money, which poses interesting selection challenges in subject areas, such as history, in which there is a great deal of interdisciplinary activity.

Economics Review

For many years, the materials in support of Northwestern University's economics department were purchased with funds from a central social science allocation. In 1998 a new fund designated solely for the support of the economics program was created. This new fund was entirely separate from allocations used to support the library's business and management collections. Shortly thereafter, the long process of determining budgetary priorities, changing the focus of the economics collection to match changes in the research needs of the department, updating the journal list, and laying the groundwork for future funding requests began. As part of this effort, a comprehensive review of the economics serials collection was initiated to document the historic shape of the collection, check titles for relevance to current departmental needs, and plan for long-range change. Because citation analysis was used as one of several review criteria, the review results were also helpful in understanding the faculty's historic and current research interests.

David Carpenter and Malcolm Getz described their comprehensive review of the economics collection at Vanderbilt University in a 1995 article.[4] Their model, which was largely quantitative, was adapted to fit NUL's situation. The NUL study concentrated only on journals, used a mix of quantitative and qualitative benchmarks, and was limited to print materials.[5] Citation analyses and rough circulation counts were used to create a list of well-cited titles that were not in NUL's collections as well as a list of undercited titles that were in the collection. These lists were then matched to faculty research interests, OCLC records were checked to see if other Illinois libraries held the material, price information was gathered, and a final list of proposed changes to the collection was created and presented to the faculty. The study ultimately resulted in the acquisition of journals that were wanted by Northwestern's economics community and the cancellation of titles that were no longer needed.[6]

Philosophy Review

In addition to the philosophy collection housed in the University Library, the philosophy department maintains a small collection of core materials in a departmental reading room that is completely separate from, and entirely independent of, NUL. In the late 1990s, several philosophy graduate students reviewed the journal collection housed in the departmental reading room. Their work led to a review of NUL's philosophy journal collection. Together with NUL, the students helped to identify duplicate titles, which led to discussions about which, if any, could be cancelled from either collection. The exercise, which was qualitative and unscientific, involved discussion, comparison of notes, and general conversations about the department, its needs, and trends in the field. As a result of this print-based review, no journals were cancelled or added to the library's collection.

History Review

The review of history serials was done to update the collection, address shifts in the research emphasis of faculty, and ensure adequate coverage of new research avenues within the discipline as a whole. In the course of the review, it became evident that the need to understand the impact of subscriptions to large electronic journal packages on collection content was also of paramount importance.

The review of NUL's history serials was extremely challenging to design and implement, partly because the journal landscape was shifting from print to electronic just as the review began and partly because history collections are intrinsically difficult to analyze. The research needs and strategies of historians vary widely. Some historians consider themselves social scientists, while others declare themselves to be humanists. Because of the hybrid nature of the discipline itself, there is a mix of quantitative and qualitative approaches to scholarship that, in turn, leads to a complex nexus of research behaviors.[7] A good research-level collection will inevitably mirror this complexity by including an enormous amount of scholarship, spanning numerous languages, and ranging in content from literary materials to quantitative works. Moreover, because the discipline itself is so diverse, there is no one best way to judge the usefulness of history journals. For example, some historians might see the validity of citation analysis as a measure of a journal's worth, while others might dismiss such methods entirely. Most historians use very large quantities of material, often including journals that may seem, to non-historians, to be relatively obscure. However, such journals may be critically important.

The History Collection

NUL's print history journal collection is scattered throughout the library system. Most history journals can be found in the library's main stacks, in the library storage facility (for backfiles), and in the periodical reading room (for many, but not all, of the library's current history journals). In addition, the Melville J. Herskovits Library of African Studies houses a large and extremely important collection of print history titles. History of science journals are housed either in the main stacks or in the Seeley G. Mudd

Library for Science and Engineering. The Pritzker Legal Research Center has a collection of legal history materials that is entirely separate, both administratively and physically, from the other history-related collections at Northwestern University. The United Library of the Garrett-Evangelical and Seabury-Western Theological Seminaries supports the history of religion.

Electronic versions of print history journals are delivered through many different services; chronological coverage varies from service to service.[8] While the funds used to pay for subscriptions to NUL's history journals are managed by several librarians, electronic packages, which may include history titles, are paid from a combination of sources but are centrally administered.

Resources for the History Serials Review

Each year, the library's serials department generates lists of print and electronic journals to which the library subscribes. These lists are sorted according to the collection fund to which the titles are charged. The lists also include titles with print subscriptions paid by subject-specific funds, but whose electronic access is paid from central funds or other sources (JSTOR journals are the prime example). Titles for which there is only electronic access through a centrally administered aggregator do not show up on the subject-specific lists (e.g., Expanded Academic ASAP, also known as EXAC) The serials department title list for the general history collection was used as the basis for the history serials review. The list included all journals, annuals, and numbered series, regardless of format, paid for with general history funds. It excluded materials on Africa, African American history, history of science, history of religion and Jewish studies, and almost all materials in Slavic languages.

Method and Scope

Major work on the history serials review began in 2003–2004, but for a variety of reasons, the project was not completed until the summer of 2005.[9] The first part of the project involved deciding which titles to include in the review and testing various evaluation methods. Circulation statistics from the library's Voyager system were recorded for all of the journals paid for by the general history fund. The library circulates journals to faculty and graduate student carrels and to the preservation department; therefore, these statistics were of limited value because they reflected only the number of times volumes of print journals were charged to a carrel by graduate students or faculty and the number of times preservation staff pulled a title from the shelf.

The next step consisted of gathering and verifying the subscription prices for the journals. Prices included print, or print plus electronic where appropriate. In 2003, when the study began, there were no subscriptions to electronic-only titles paid for with general history funds. Finally, the list was sorted into categories: foreign language titles, titles that could be considered monographic series and any titles with ISBNs, and titles that had electronic versions. The original intention was to review each of these categories.

Between 2003 and 2005, when the study was completed, new bundled packages and service providers were added to NUL's collections, more foreign language titles came online, and five new subscriptions were added to the library's general history collection. There were no cancellations during this period. Because the number of history journals available in electronic format increased, an assessment of the extent of the library's electronic history journal holdings was included in the 2005 review.[10]

At the start of the project, use of citation analysis, a method that worked well for the economics review, was tried and in early January 2005, two Journal Citation Reports (JCRs) were created, a Journal Summary List/History of Social Science and a Journal Summary List/History. The latter listed fifteen journals with the highest impact factors; of these, all but one was in the NUL collection; the one title not held by NUL was available in the Chicago area. Given the size of NUL's history serials list, the fact that many important titles held by NUL were not part of this review (e.g., journals devoted to African history and history of science), the limited time and resources available to conduct the review, as well as the unsurprising results revealed by the two JCRs, it was determined that the amount of work required to do a proper citation analysis would not yield any enlightening results. Consequently, citation analysis as a viable tool for the history evaluation was abandoned.[11]

The next step consisted of reassessing and consolidating the original title lists. In this phase, extensive work was done on the list of electronic titles and the following categories of material were excluded from the final study:

- any titles with ISBNs and any numbered series titles;
- most membership fees;
- most journals in Slavic languages;
- journals concerning the African continent;
- history of science journals;
- history of religion journals;

- African American history titles; and
- Jewish studies journals.

Included in the final study were the five new subscriptions in general history that had been added since compilation of the original list in 2003 and all titles with ISSNs that appeared on the general history list prepared by the serials department. The final list included 372 titles.

Each title was examined for currency (Had the subscription lapsed but nonetheless remained as an active record in Voyager?) and checked for electronic editions (Was there an electronic version that was included with the cost of print, available through an aggregator, or was an electronic version freely available?). Circulation statistics for print titles were revisited. However, usage statistics were not compiled for electronic titles. Of the 131 journals that were determined to be electronically available at the time of the study, 76 were delivered by two or more services and had multiple coverage years, making it cumbersome to gather usage statistics (table 1). More significantly, the 76 titles represent those that are important enough to be considered permanent parts of the collection. Most history titles that might be considered marginal to NUL's collection do not have electronic versions; the few that do have appeared in electronic form so recently that any available usage data would not have historical significance.

TABLE 1
Number of Electronically Available History Titles Covered
by One or More Services (Coverage Dates Not Distinguished)

NUMBER OF SERVICES	NUMBER OF TITLES
1	55
2	36
3	29
4	10
5	1

Foreign Language Titles

To determine if the breakdown of foreign language journals matched the current needs of the history department, the journals included in the study were divided into language groups. More than 60 percent of the titles are English-language or multilingual (with one language being English). Not surprisingly, given the historic scope of NUL's collection, the majority of foreign language titles are in French and German. At first glance, the results of the analysis suggested that foreign language coverage in Spanish, Portuguese, Slavic languages, and Asian languages is scant; however, this is misleading because Slavic language titles and all journals pertaining to the study of the African continent, many of which are in French, Spanish, and Portuguese, were excluded from the study.

Print Titles

The circulation statistics of print titles were reviewed. This proved to be labor-intensive and did not yield much helpful information. Because of the library's limited circulation policy, statistics could only suggest what might be peripheral to NUL's collecting mission, and thus, had to be combined with subjective knowledge of the library's historic collection strengths and weaknesses as well as general knowledge of the discipline. Furthermore, society membership dues posed unique problems. Some memberships include a journal and a newsletter, while others include only a newsletter. Society memberships were included for this part of the study only if the membership fee clearly included a journal subscription. In the end, twelve titles and one society membership were identified as possibly marginal.

Electronic Lists

Updating and analyzing the list of history journals with electronic versions was the most time consuming and complicated part of the study. The concept of a self-contained list of history serials proved to be almost antiquated; in fact, history serials are acquired under so many rubrics that it is virtually impossible to obtain an integrated list and, accordingly, a clear sense of the total cost of the history collection. The following steps were required to analyze the electronic journals:

1. Based on the master list of 372 titles created initially in 2003, a list of 91 journals with electronic versions was created. The list was then updated to see if any titles had added e-versions since 2003; however, no attempt was made to check the completeness of content of the e-versions. By 2005, the number of titles with e-versions had grown to 131 (an increase of approximately 44 percent).
2. The delivery method for each title on the electronic list was identified.

3. Titles with coverage in multiple services were identified. The years of coverage for each service were recorded, although completeness of content was not checked.
4. The number of non-English-language titles delivered by multiple services was identified. Non-English-language titles with electronic versions were also identified.[12]

From 2003 through summer 2005, a significant number of electronic titles were added to the library's collection as a result of aggregator packages and other electronic providers. The revised e-journal list also included journals freely available from foreign sources, such as the French-language site Gallica (http://gallica.bnf.fr/) for older materials, and Persée (www.persee.fr/).

A perusal of electronically available titles indicated that a full compilation of usage statistics, in cases where statistics were available, would not yield any recommendations for cancellation of current content because the titles with electronic versions are central to the collecting mission of the library. However, the list under review included only those titles that have print versions that are paid for by history funds. It did not include titles that come to the library as part of big deals.

Results of the Study and Further Recommendations

The study produced several concrete results. First, when the lists were examined for duplicative electronic delivery, it was discovered that many journals were delivered by multiple services. (In some cases, one service might provide backfiles, while another would provide current content.) Second, open access and freely available links to foreign language journals, particularly backfiles, were discovered, and, in some cases, it was recommended that OPAC links for these titles be added if possible. Third, the print list was examined to identify titles appropriate for cancellation, and based on circulation statistics, subjective knowledge of departmental priorities, and problems with responses to claim requests, twelve titles were identified. Of those, one title was cancelled in 2006 and the other eleven are being retained for the time being, but will be considered for possible cancellation in the future. A by-product of the study was the discovery of some instances of incorrect assignment of funds, and titles that needed to be claimed.

Overall, the intricacies of electronic materials available to the NUL history community made it difficult to mange the resources effectively. It was frequently unclear on what basis a title was being received, why titles came from multiple sources, how the electronic materials related to their print counterparts, or what was available for free versus what was received on the basis of a payment. It may be that another in-depth study of history journals should be undertaken with the following goals:

1. Assess the impact of the purchase of electronic packages on the library's history collection, including review of the names and number of titles that are acquired as part of a package rather than being selected individually for addition to the collection.
2. Determine the approximate cost of electronic versions of each history journal for which an electronic version is available.
3. Determine the overlap in coverage dates for titles with multiple delivery services.
4. Determine whether some electronic versions can be cancelled.
5. Determine the extent of freely available/open access history journals, particularly for foreign language titles.
6. Examine the feasibility and usefulness of compiling interlibrary loan statistics for journal evaluation purposes.

Comments on Review Methods and Conclusions

Implications of the Big Deal for History Collections

The full impact of big deals on the cost, shape, and scope of NUL's history serials collection has yet to be fully realized. Inevitably, as more and more history titles come online, costs for dual formats (print and electronic) continue to climb, and aggregated packages reshape the journal landscape, history journal collections will change. Libraries will no longer be able to afford both print and electronic versions of history titles. But what about the smaller, relatively obscure, print-only journals that are so important to history collections? Will librarians be forced to cancel such titles in order to free up collection dollars to fund aggregated packages that may be generally worthwhile but may also include titles that are peripheral to the library's research and teaching missions? When libraries subscribe to, or otherwise acquire, large packages of electronic journals, they must often take every title offered by the package vendors. These journals enter the collection at a *bargain* price. But are such acquisitions really bargains? Librarians might be wise to total the cost of all unsubscribed titles in a package offer to see what hidden costs might be involved in signing on to a big deal?[13] While this is an issue for all collections, it is particularly profound for history because many important titles are low usage. What, then, constitutes a *good* history collection in the new environment? Is it a collection with many titles provided by an aggregator, or one that continues to include relatively obscure, perhaps print-only, publications?

Usage Statistics

Usage statistics refer here to the statistics provided by a vendor or publisher on the number of times a journal has been accessed electronically by an authorized user.[14] Although such statistics generally are an excellent collection management tool, for low-usage history titles, usage is not always an indicator of a journal's merit. Titles that have been carefully selected for inclusion in a history collection are more likely to become cancellation candidates for subjective reasons, such as changes in the research and teaching mission of the university. While it might be interesting to see usage statistics for nonselected history titles (i.e., titles that come as part of a big-deal package), it is doubtful that low usage for one or two titles in a larger package will result in canceling the entire package.[15]

Problems of Developing Review Methods and Comparisons with Other Serials Reviews

Methods used by any academic library undertaking a comprehensive history journal collection review will depend on a number of factors: the ways in which funds are managed and distributed, the extent of foreign language holdings, the faith historians put in citation analysis as an accurate benchmark of journal usage, the mix of electronic and print titles, the validity of circulation counts, the availability and usefulness of usage statistics, and the extent to which the history selector has control over additions to the collection in light of vendor policies on acquiring titles as part of big-deal subscriptions. Staff expertise in evaluation techniques and staff time are also critical. It is not necessary to have sophisticated statistical skills to evaluate a history collection, but it is critical to understand local needs, the peculiarities of the discipline, and the delicacy of the balance between subscribing to low-use selected titles and titles that come to the library through aggregated packages.

Certain review methods are more useful in some disciplines than others. For example, citation analyses and ISI impact factors might be more helpful in an assessment of economics journals than in reviewing journals in philosophy or history, while consultation with faculty on cancellation decisions is critical across the board. However, the unfolding complexities of NUL's history serials review affirmed that the introduction of electronic journals has so profoundly changed the serials landscape that review method comparisons with previous journal reviews and with reviews across disciplines yields little that is enlightening. Future serials reviews in social science and humanities disciplines will need to look only fleetingly to past studies for inspiration. New models are emerging that include assessments of the impact of bundling and big deals, analysis of usage statistics, licensing terms, ease of use, and cancellation of print. Indeed, there are some indications that librarians may need to measure usage in the new environment on an article-by-article basis, rather than by measuring journal access.[16] In addition to these cross-disciplinary issues, librarians will continue to be mindful not only of the research behaviors of a given discipline but how these behaviors are shifting to take advantage of the enormous power of technology.

The fund manager's knowledge of a given discipline and the faculty's research and teaching needs remain the best and most accurate determinate of a collection's currency.[17] Yet, as aggregated, centrally administered serials packages continue to change the contours of carefully-selected, discipline-based journal collections, librarians are faced with the need to ask new sets of questions about their journals: questions about duplication, delivery mechanisms, and payment models. In the final analysis, selectors across all social science and humanities disciplines who wish to review their collections will be faced with multiple formats, multiple vendors, the acquisition of titles that might not be otherwise added to a collection, as well as the need to manage traditional print-based journals that might be available in only one format. The new models require new methods, new ways of thinking, and a careful walk through a whole new landscape.

REFERENCE NOTES

1. Halcyon R. Enssle and Michelle L. Wilde, "So You Have to Cancel Journals? Statistics That Help," *Library Collections, Acquisitions, & Technical Services* 26 (2002): 260, notes that F. W. Lancaster, "Evaluating Collections by Their Use," *Collection Management* 4, no. 1/2 (1982): 15–44, ". . . delineates the problems and limitations of three approaches to evaluating library collections: subjective evaluation by subject specialists; checking against external benchmarks, and measurement by volume and type of use." Regina C. McBride and Kathlyn Behm, "A Journal Usage Study in an Academic Library: Evaluation of Selected Criteria," *Serials Librarian* 45, no. 3 (2003): 26–27; Sanna Talja and Hanni Maula, "Reasons for the Use and Nonuse of Electronic Journals and Databases: A Domain Analytic Study in Four Scholarly Disciplines," *Journal of Documentation* 59, no. 6 (2003): 685–87.
2. Charles W. Bailey, Jr., *The Open Access Bibliography: Liberating Scholarly Literature with E-prints and Open Access Journals* (Washington, D.C.: ARL, 2005), www.escholarlypub.com/oab/oab.pdf, www.escholarlypub.com/oab/oab.htm (accessed 3 September 2006). Bailey notes that there are various definitions of open access. For his bibliography, he uses the Budapest Open Access Initiative definition:

The literature that should be freely accessible online is that which scholars give to the world without expectation of payment. Primarily, this category encompasses their peer-reviewed journal articles, but it also includes any unreviewed preprints that they might wish to put online for comment or to alert colleagues to important research findings. There are many degrees and kinds of wider and easier access to this literature. By "open access" to this literature, we mean its free availability on the public Internet, permitting any users to read, download, copy, distribute print, search, or link to the full texts of these articles, crawl them for indexing, pass them as data to software, or use them for any other lawful purpose, without financial, legal, or technical barriers other than those inseparable from gaining access to the Internet itself. The only constraint on reproduction and distribution, and the only role for copyright in this domain, should be to give authors control over the integrity of their work and the right to be properly acknowledged and cited, 11.

This definition is widely used, but it is not the only one. See, for example, Edward M. Corrado, "The Importance of Open Access, Open Source, and Open Standards for Libraries," *Issues in Science and Technology Librarianship* 42 (Spring 2005), www.istl.org/05-spring/article2.html (accessed 3 September 2006). Corrado states that "open access basically calls for scholarly publications to be made freely available to libraries and end users." Also note that an enormous amount of literature on open access has recently appeared. For literature reviews on, among other things, open access, see Lauren E. Corbett, "Serials: Review of the Literature 2000–2003," *Library Resources & Technical Services* 50, no. 1 (January 2006): 16–30. For guides to repositories, see the Directory of Open Access Repositories (OpenDOAR), www.opendoar.org (accessed 19 October 2006), and the Registry of Open Access Repositories (ROAR), http://archives.eprints.org (accessed 19 October 2006).

3. Qiana Johnson, "User Preferences in Formats of Print and Electronic Journals," *Collection Building* 23, no. 2 (2004): 76; Donald W. King et al., "Library Economic Metrics: Examples of the Comparison of Electronic and Print Journal Collections and Collection Services," *Library Trends* 51, no. 3 (Winter 2003): 389; for new challenges to bibliographers, see Krista D. Schmidt, Pongracz Sennyey, and Timothy V. Carstens's "New Roles for a Changing Environment: Implications of Open Access for Libraries," *College & Research Libraries* 66, no. 5 (September 2005): 411; Steve Black, "Impact of Full Text on Print Journal Use at a Liberal Arts College," *Library Resources & Technical Services* 49, no. 1 (January 2005): 20, 24–25; Talja and Maula, "Reasons for Use and Non-use of Electronic Journals and Databases," 685–87.

4. David Carpenter and Malcolm Getz, "Evaluation of Library Resources in the Field of Economics: A Case Study," *Collection Management* 20, no. 1/2 (1995): 49–89.

5. Work on the NUL economics review was done with student help. The author wishes to thank the Office of the Provost, Northwestern University, for a grant to hire a student under the auspices of the Residential College Research Assistant program. Sabina Manilov, WCAS '01, was instrumental in the economics serials review.

6. The review methods and results of the study can be found in Harriet Lightman with Sabina Manilov, "A Simple Method for Evaluating a Journal Collection: A Case Study of Northwestern University Library's Economics Collection," *Journal of Academic Librarianship* 26, no. 3 (May 2000): 183–90.

7. Margaret Stieg Dalton and Laurie Charnigo, "Historians and Their Information Sources," *College & Research Libraries* 65, no. 5 (September 2004): 400–425; Roberto Delgadillo and Beverly P. Lynch, "Future Historians: Their Quest for

Information," *College & Research Libraries* 60, no. 3 (May 1999): 245–59; Talja and Maula, "Reasons for the Use and Non-use," 675–78. On issues concerning early adoption of electronic journals by historians, see Harriet Lightman, "On Libraries: Some Thoughts about Electronic Journals," *Historically Speaking* II, no. 3 (May 2001): 13–14.

8. In addition to a rich collection of print titles, NUL has long held subscriptions to JSTOR, Project Muse, and Expanded Academic ASAP (EXAC). Within the last few years, the library has also invested in other large electronic packages.

9. Northwestern University undergraduate Elizabeth Aronson did preliminary work in 2001–2002. Jessica Joslin, SESP '06, was instrumental in the history serials review during the academic year 2003–2004 and created most of the charts on which the final analyses were based. The author wishes to thank the Office of the Provost, Northwestern University for grants to hire both students under the auspices of the Residential College Research Assistant program.

10. Numbered monographic series were excluded from the final review.

11. On the limits of Journal Citation Reports, see Enssle and Wilde, "So You Have to Cancel Journals," 266.

12. At the time of the history serials evaluation, relatively few foreign language titles were available online. French-language titles were the most readily available, with three subscribed titles being available through vendor or publisher sites and six being freely available. The number of German-language titles available online was small because, at the time of this study, the library did not yet subscribe to DigiZeitschriften (www.digizeitschriften.de/), the German-language online journal archive (accessed 3 September 2006).

13. See Schmidt, Sennyey, and Carstens, "New Roles for a Changing Environment," 410–11; Thomas A. Peters, "What's the Big Deal?" *Journal of Academic Librarianship* 27, no. 4 (July 2001) 302–304. Peters suggests that more analysis of costs awaits collections librarians:

> Despite the furious activities of academic library consortia throughout the 1990s to negotiate both big and lesser deals, the real revolution in collection development has not yet occurred. The real revolution will unfold when everyone in the value chain performs a cost-benefit analysis of each link, 303.

For a summary of recent studies of cost-benefit comparison, see King et al., "Economic Metrics," 382–83.

14. King et al., "Economic Metrics," 380, notes that "*usage* [is measured] in terms of the use of information provided by the library service such as the information content of an article that is read from access to the electronic collection." See their lengthy discussion of usage measurements on pages 380–82.

15. For an excellent overview of the issues, see Enssle and Wilde, "So You Have to Cancel Journals," 261.

16. King et al., "Economic Metrics," 380.

17. Schmidt, Sennyey, and Carstens, "New Roles for a Changing Environment," 411.

Reference Serials Management in the Digital Library

JEAN M. ALEXANDER

The management of reference serials, although in some respects similar to that of other serials, has a number of unique characteristics that are worth highlighting. The following discussion of reference serials management draws upon the experience of the Hunt Library Reference Department at the Carnegie Mellon University Libraries (CMUL) in Pittsburgh, Pennsylvania. Although inevitably reflective of the particular context of one mid-size research library, CMUL's experience has much in common with that of other academic libraries. This discussion concentrates on broad patterns and issues rather than specific products, tools, or technologies that would be quickly outdated. The author hopes this overview can serve as a stimulus for thought and future direction for reference librarians in libraries of all types.

Purpose of Reference Serials

Reference serials were first affected by computerization more than forty years ago with the advent of online bibliographic databases and library catalogs. Further waves of change came with CD-ROMs, remote end-user searching, and the growth of the Web. Many print serials have been cancelled, ceased publication, migrated to the Internet, or been marginalized. Electronic indexing and abstracting services have added full-text content, making it difficult to distinguish reference sources from general collections. For many students and faculty, reference serials have become completely irrelevant: Google or Yahoo! is now their catalog or index of choice. Google

Scholar threatens to put federated searching tools and possibly even licensed subject databases out of business. Do reference serials have a future? To answer that question, it is best to begin by defining the basic purpose of the reference serial.

A reference serial can be defined as a publication issued in parts on a regular basis and used for reference purposes or housed in a physical or virtual reference collection. Examples of reference serials include directories, indexes, abstracts, bibliographies, digests, statistical series, data, legislation, legal cases and compilations of facts. These are the types of reference serials traditionally collected, but it is also useful to consider functional definitions centered on user needs. What purposes do reference serials serve?

The most obvious purpose is currency. Certain reference serials refresh information through revision. Others supply new information that supplements a previous publication by the addition of recent facts or events. The regular periodicity of the serial serves as a marker of the limits of revision or addition, as the case may be. Because information overload may be a problem for scholars, reference serials help organize and digest new information for scanning and current awareness.

Serial publications also developed to meet the needs of publishers for a guaranteed return on their initial capital investment and a long-term commitment to sustain publication. The benefit for the subscriber is long-term access to a familiar and valued research tool. In addition, serial publication plays a practical role in organizing the publication and distribution process.

Apart from currency and periodicity, what needs are met by reference serials? As these serials accumulate, they come to form a comprehensive chronological record of human knowledge organized in ways that are useful for specific purposes. One of these purposes is representational; reference sources act as surrogates and pointers. They help researchers to understand and assess information resources by describing, summarizing, and evaluating them and indicating where the resources can be found. In addition, reference sources also help users discover previously unknown items, but this function is sometimes overemphasized from the user's point of view.[1]

Different functionalities of reference serials may be in conflict. For example, the desire for comprehensive coverage may conflict with the desire for a pointer to the location of the full text. According to a recent estimate by Carol Tenopir, only one-fourth to one-third of scholarly periodicals published worldwide is available in electronic format.[2] Whether access to the actual materials is readily available, the need for bibliographic information on print publications and archival resources continues. Reference information should not be reduced to the lowest common denominator, and it may be necessary at times to explain this principle to the public and library administrators.

The purposes served by reference serials are as important as ever, which is why search engine developers have been scrambling to satisfy old needs in new ways. For example, popular e-mail updates from Web news sources mimic the selective dissemination of information (SDI) services offered by online databases to meet the scholar's need for currency in an online environment. The question is not whether reference serials have a future, but rather, what form will they take in the future and how will they be funded and used? However, before speculating on the future, there needs to be an understanding of the situation as it exists today.

Reference Serials Collections

In North American libraries, the debate that raged for years over retention of print reference subscriptions seems to have been settled largely in favor of cancellation of print.[3] Initial concerns about discrepancies in content, interrupted access, and preservation of electronic resources have been overridden for pragmatic reasons. Some print looseleaf services and reference serials remain viable, perhaps because individual subscribers and public and special libraries prefer them for reasons of personal convenience or cost. Even academic libraries sometimes choose to retain a few duplicate print subscriptions of such resources as directories, statistical sources, annuals, or atlases due to their ease of access and superior display capabilities. On the other hand, CD-ROMs have proven to be a transitional format for reference departments because of the resources' access limitations and technical complications.

As print, microform, and CD-ROM formats decline in importance, there is a fear that popular Web-based databases will crowd out more specialized resources, but it is difficult to gauge whether this is actually happening. Many reference serials have gone to electronic-only publication, but there are no precise statistics on this development. Others have ceased publication altogether due to competition, and again, no accurate count of these exists, especially because there are other explanations for the termination of a serial. It is not possible to predict how many smaller publishers will be driven out of the electronic market by the dominance of a few large publishers and the resultant loss of resource breadth and depth. There has probably been a net gain in diversity with the growth of the free Web, but in certain fields, there may well be a need to protect endangered publications by continuing to subscribe to them, whether in print or electronically.

For a rough-and-ready snapshot of Web database collections in academic libraries, the author compared the CMUL's online subscription database list with those of five peer institutions: three Association of Research Libraries (ARL) and two non-ARL libraries.[4] Total library materials expenditures at these libraries varied by a factor of five and spending per full-time equivalent (FTE) student by a factor of four. Expenditures for current serial subscriptions at the six libraries varied by a factor of five, and electronic serials expenditures by a factor of three.[5] Yet with regard to subscription databases, the variance was less; the smallest number of databases was 145, the largest 246. A research library with a small budget spends a larger portion of that budget on reference serials in order to support basic needs.

Of the reference databases held at the six libraries, approximately 3 percent of the databases were held by all six libraries, 5 percent were held by five libraries, and 5 percent were held by four libraries, suggesting that a core collection of academic reference databases exists that constitutes at least 13 percent of total titles (undoubtedly a much higher percentage when measured in dollars, but that data was not readily available). The common core titles include such standard databases as Web of Science, PsycINFO, LexisNexis Academic, MLA, Inspec, and Encyclopædia Britannica Online.

It was also interesting to see how many unique database titles each library licensed. Unique titles ranged from 8 to 40 percent, with most in the area of 20 to 30 percent. For this part of the study one non-U.S. institution, Cambridge University, was added to the mix with 29 percent unique titles. The unique holdings of the seven libraries were of all types: specialized subject indexes, data sets, full-text literary collections, retrospective indexes, business databases, and ready reference sources. Without overinterpreting this informal survey, the information suggests that there is considerable uniformity in reference serial collections. How do academic libraries decide which reference serials to obtain and which to cancel?

The Collection Management Process

Ideally, collection management should take place within a matrix of fixed policies, goals, and procedures; however, the framework for decision making refuses to stand still. The reference department—and even the library as a whole—has only partial control over its own collections due to consortial purchasing, mergers and acquisitions of vendor products, bundling of contents, changes in content of aggregator databases (exacerbated by the unfortunate trend for journal publishers to withdraw and set up separate publisher databases), and changes in government documents provision (ERIC is one example).

In a university library, one or more reference departments may each have their own serials budget, but as reference serials merge with full-text journals and books, reference expenditures become difficult to isolate. In the early years of digital library collections, a library-wide committee was often charged with selecting databases, sometimes under the supervision of a digital collections librarian. But now that digital collections have become the norm, and technical requirements less onerous, selection responsibility is likely to be shared among a number of individuals or departments, including reference departments, subject specialists, and administrators. The budget and final decision-making authority may be centralized, but input is distributed. When questions are raised about the value of and demand for a particular database, decisions are often deferred to the selector or department with the most subject expertise. At the CMUL, this process is documented in archives of e-mails, committee minutes, and database records going back several years.

The practical management of reference serials is similar to that of other serials in that it represents an ongoing commitment of money, space, and time. As more and more reference monographs, such as encyclopedias and dictionaries, are transformed into electronic serials (at least in the budgetary sense), libraries incur additional ongoing commitments. However, unlike other serials, reference serials usually need to be renewed, and hence, reviewed in some way, on an annual basis. How is this process handled?

Academic library budgets exist within an institutional budget, supplemented to varying degrees by other funds, such as endowments and gifts. In theory, a library should review its list of database subscriptions each year, but in practice, truly holistic reviews occur only under extreme budget pressure. These reviews absorb an enormous amount of time and effort from librarians and faculty, who cannot be expected to go through the process every year. Other hindrances to a comprehensive review of reference databases revolve around the fact that some databases are acquired under multiyear contracts, and not all databases are renewed in parallel with a library's fiscal year, but may be renewed at different times throughout the year. New databases are aggressively marketed with time-sensitive discounts, forcing ad hoc trials and purchases. New subscriptions tend to be sponsored by a subject specialist or department, often with the expectation that equivalent cost savings will be realized through cancellations or reallocation of existing funds. If the database is interdisciplinary, several library departments may be asked to contribute and funds must then be transferred from specific subject budgets to a central database account.[6]

To maintain purchasing power, this database fund, like other journal funds, has to be infused with additional money each year, often at the expense of monographs or other library needs. When the situation becomes untenable, the library undertakes a large cancellation project, which may encompass serials across the board. CMUL last conducted such a project in 2003, resulting in the cancellation of approximately $17,000 worth of reference indexes and electronic databases. After extensive consultation with academic departments, analysis of usage data, and internal discussion among librarians, a list of suggested cancellations was posted on the library Web site for feedback. There was relatively little feedback on reference databases, and while all comments received a personal response, no decision on a database cancellation was changed due to objections from an individual faculty member or student.

Selection and Evaluation Criteria

Each library's collection should to be shaped and evaluated on the basis of an overall collection policy reflecting its mission.[7] However, such policies go only so far towards helping librarians make difficult decisions, particularly when choosing among several high-priority resources that fall within the institution's policy and mission, and more specific evaluation techniques are needed.

Shaping a collection of electronic reference serials is an ongoing activity in which users (faculty and, in some cases, students) are invited to participate. Users are kept in the loop not only during major cancellation projects but throughout the lifecycle of a database subscription. Some library Web sites highlight trial databases, new databases, and databases targeted for possible cancellation. Libraries recognize that a database may show low use because it is "invisible" to users, not necessarily because it is unwanted. While most librarians consult with faculty before canceling reference databases, it would be unrealistic to expect such consultation to settle the really thorny conflicts that arise.[8] As for the evaluation of new candidates for acquisition, a surfeit of trials may exhaust the already limited pool of willing faculty participants. If faculty feedback is essential for a new acquisition, it helps to frame the request in terms of trade-offs or cost to prevent the kind of automatic "good will" support of the library that helps not a whit with decision making. On the other hand, a detailed and persuasive request for a new database coming from a department or group of faculty carries considerable weight.

In the print era, cancellations of reference serials seldom required such broad consultation. According to CMUL records, the reason for cancellation of a print reference serial was always financial, but had to be justified or approved. Typical justifications included the existence of duplicates, low use, replacement by other resources (including resources on the Web), or availability at another local library.[9] As more and more libraries move towards electronic-only collections that require authentication even for in-library use, regional holdings of a reference title become less relevant to selection and cancellation decisions.

General rules of thumb can help to some extent with cancellation decisions. All other things being equal, users prefer unity and simplicity. *Unity* implies that the whole resource is available in one place. When a reference source such as a catalog or index is divided by format or location, the portion that is smaller or less convenient to access often falls into disuse. For example, users tend to avoid card catalogs once a substantial proportion of the catalog is available online. Similarly, users prefer that the entire date range of an index be available online, rather than face the inconvenience of using certain volumes in print. *Simplicity* implies that the resource is easy to use, a merit that numerous user studies and focus groups have identified as a high priority. Good interface design, intuitive navigation, and clear definition of scope and content all enhance the user's perception that a resource is easy to use. At one time, libraries were concerned that a proliferation of electronic products from multiple vendors with different interfaces would be confusing to users. This concern is far less prevalent today, but there may still be a slight preference for acquiring several databases from the same vendor for the sake of a common interface, the ability to search and save across databases, and the practical advantage of having to deal with fewer vendors for purposes of acquisitions or maintenance.

Users also prefer an unobstructed pathway through all phases of the research process, from discovery to full-text documents to data storage, writing, and publication. Librarians have learned to view library research as part of a continuum, rather than an isolated act. This does not necessarily mean that the full-text document must be immediately obtained. Users seem willing to wait for the text to be delivered as long as they are able to complete a delivery request, as demonstrated by their satisfaction with document delivery, interlibrary loan, and such e-retailers as Amazon.com and Barnes & Noble.com. If a full-text document is immediately available, users expect to be able to save or reformat the text in a way that meets their needs and facilitates the next stage of their project. A database that enables links to full-text documents, integrates easily with bibliographic software, and allows unrestricted use of the contents will find favor with reference selectors. Consequently, publishers and vendors have been quick to provide these kinds of enhancements, which increase their competitiveness in the reference market. Other features, such as customizability, availability of MARC records, and availability of PDFs, are advantageous but their absence is not necessarily a deal breaker if the database is strongly needed and desired by students and faculty.

An analysis of comparative usage data gathered over a substantial period of time between databases and between libraries is essential. For some time, libraries have been asking vendors to supply standardized data on session and query details following International Coalition of Library Consortia guidelines, so that evaluation can be more reliable. In their 2001 article, Blecic, Fiscella, and Wiberley pointed out some of the problems and pitfalls of usage data, especially when it is interpreted in a cursory way.[10] They stress the need to look at monthly, or even daily, usage data and to wait for multiyear data before drawing conclusions about a product's usefulness. The authors also recommended national reporting of per-capita use of databases for the purpose of comparison with other libraries. Lee also stresses the importance of detailed usage data, while cautioning that use statistics do not always reflect the value of a resource. He recommends that at least one other evaluative technique, such as consultation with users, should be combined with usage data.[11] Experience at CMUL suggests that even the most reliable data can only be helpful within an interpretive context that leads to action. Usage data are a blunt tool for comparing databases of widely differing content, constituency, and price. Formulae can be devised to take these other factors into account, but formula-based fund allocations have often proved difficult to apply.

Technical Services and Processing Perspectives

Digital reference serials have complicated acquisitions and cataloging, increasing the need for communication between public and technical services.[12] The number of individual vendors that must be entered into the university purchasing system has proliferated. Each electronic reference subscription must be tracked according to an individual renewal timetable. The library's integrated management system may not be able to handle all aspects of electronic serials management, which often leads to the creation of in-house databases that may be awkward and difficult to use, especially for staff outside of the department that created or uses the databases on a regular basis. Confusion and miscommunication can cause errors. Licenses not renewed by the renewal date may lead to loss of access, a lapse that might not be detected until users report a problem. At that point, staff must try to troubleshoot the problem, which may be due to technical difficulties at the supplier end, network complications, computer troubles within the library system, or authentication or licensing issues. Clear lines of communication and assignment of responsibility for resolving such service interruptions are needed.

Library staff, often in acquisitions, regularly handle licensing contracts, frequently in consultation with campus legal counsel. Annual contract renewals require consultation with reference staff, a process that has become more streamlined in recent years, but may still delay or occasionally interfere with access to a database. Large suppliers of databases usually give adequate notice of price increases, which may vary greatly from year to year, and tend to allow cancellation windows of thirty to ninety days, during which time consultation and decision making must take place. Most libraries rarely have an opportunity to negotiate prices, although they may feel obligated to try. Much staff time is devoted to establishing and updating IP ranges for authentication, a process often complicated when distance learning sites are factored into the agreement. Reference serials are only a small part of the electronic serials acquisition picture, which has become so complex that electronic resources management systems are a hot topic in acquisitions circles.

Staff members with responsibility for cataloging electronic reference serials also report that their jobs have changed. When CD-ROM reference databases predominated, cataloging issues were minor; the labeling and storage of CD-ROMs may have been managed within the reference department and a list of databases was relatively easy to maintain. In the past, serials catalogers were sometimes left out of the planning process and not notified in advance of new acquisitions. At present, catalogers are involved in adding bibliographic and holdings records to the library catalog for electronic serials and databases. In some institutions, they may work with public services librarians to implement and maintain linking tools and to revise catalog records retrospectively. (Catalogers sometimes have to scramble in surprising ways to clean up records; for example, at CMUL, older serials lacking ISSNs have had to be recataloged for use with a URL linking tool.)

The role of the catalog in the overall information universe may be unclear. Under what circumstances should free Web URLs be added to catalog records? Should these only be added when specifically requested by subject or reference librarians? Holdings records may be incomplete or inconsistent. Cataloging practice may affect the interface with such bibliographic utilities as OCLC and thereby impact interlibrary loan and document delivery. With so many new responsibilities, serials and cataloging departments may feel overwhelmed by the pace of change and the lack of a clear direction. Reduced attention to the processing of print collections, such as the trend away from check-in of paper, is a partial compensation or reaction. Within the reference department itself, staff members who once were dedicated to maintenance of the print collections are reassigned and retrained for other responsibilities.

The acquisition and cataloging of a reference database is only the beginning of making the database fully available and useful. The database has to be announced and publicized, listed and described on the library Web site in a variety of ways, and added to subject guides, class pages, and instructional materials. All these activities must be repeated when a database undergoes a change in name, URL, functionality, or content. Some of these tasks may be performed by a library webmaster or public relations officer, others by reference and instruction librarians, and perhaps others by information technology staff or catalogers. Good communication, training, and clear procedures are needed to keep up with this workload, especially due to its irregular nature. Some libraries have tried to streamline the process by creating a database of databases for storing and updating internal metadata on databases. Despite all of these efforts, students and faculty continue to have difficulty finding and selecting among the library's scholarly databases.[13]

Storage and Preservation Issues

In 2003 OCLC conducted an environmental scan and found that libraries had begun to question their traditional curatorial role.[14] OCLC's call for shared preservation is hardly surprising; solutions to electronic storage and preservation are largely beyond the control of any individual library. The specific issues for reference—which, in a nutshell, relate to the impermanence of electronic texts—are masterfully summed up in an article by Fisher, aptly titled "Now You See It; Now You Don't: The Elusive Nature of Electronic Information." Electronic documents are moving targets that confound the fundamental reference tasks of describing, organizing, summarizing, evaluating, and locating information resources. Fisher says that "if we want better retrieval and archiving of digitally created information, we need to work with those creating this information to develop new or revised bibliographic structures that can be embedded into the process of publishing and editing this digital content."[15] A tall order given the unregulated arena of digital publishing.

On a more familiar level, libraries continue to deal with the disposition and preservation of collections of print reference serials, some or all of which are also available digitally. Just as in the predigital era, each individual library decides, based on its mission and available space, whether to retain backruns of reference serials for preservation or research purposes. Most libraries continue to rely on large research libraries for the preservation of these titles. The Center for Research Libraries also serves as a national repository for rarely used materials, and regional consortia, such as the Information Alliance, comprising the libraries of the University of Kentucky, the University of Tennessee, Knoxville, and Vanderbilt University, have sprung up to share responsibility for storing and delivering rarely used print references. Many academic libraries now have their own offsite storage repositories so that each reference department decides for itself which print materials to retain onsite and which to send to offsite storage or withdraw from the collections. What factors affect these decisions?

Because many reference serials serve as finding aids, presumably they should be available for immediate consultation and browsing. On the other hand, print indexes and bibliographies are rarely used nowadays and are prime candidates for weeding or removal to offsite storage. Assuming that an archival print copy is readily accessible, it may make sense for an individual library to discard reference indexes and abstracts that are electronically available or—if this seems too drastic—move them to offsite storage. Print backfiles of indexes and abstracts that are not available electronically should probably be retained onsite unless their coverage is substantially duplicated by an alternative electronic product. Vendors should be encouraged to digitize these backfiles, and libraries should strive to purchase them whenever possible.

The disposition of other types of reference serials should be decided on a case-by-case basis. Here the distinction between serials that revise and those that supplement information comes into play. In the case of serials that revise information, such as directories, it could be argued that backfiles are only needed by the occasional historian. In the case of serials that supplement information, such as annuals, fact books, statistical series, the value of any part depends on access to the entire longitudinal series, and this type of material is best kept together as a set regardless of location. At CMUL, the latest volume is usually housed onsite for researchers to examine and help them decide whether to order additional volumes from offsite storage. All these decisions have a ripple effect on shelving and retrieval and on cataloging and circulation staff, so communication beyond the bounds of the reference department is important.

Reference Serials and the Open Web

This discussion has concentrated on reference serials as part of library collections, but all along there has been an elephant in the room. Usage data for licensed reference serials, even if perfectly consistent, tells little about their comparative value vis-à-vis scholarly resources on the open Web. Yet it is known that students and faculty rely heavily on the Web for reference purposes, and reference librarians increasingly do so as well. *Academic and Scholar Search Engines and Sources*, a guide maintained by Marcus P. Zillman, lists an impressive assortment of open access reference sources, many of them modeled after traditional reference tools.[16] These include directories; encyclopedias, such as Wikipedia; collections of reference books collections of online reference books, such as Answers.com; specialized search engines offering clustering, linking, visual display, translation, and citation searching; searchable full-text collections, such as open access journals, e-prints, dissertations, data sets, government documents, institutional repositories, digital archives; search engines for the deep Web; PDF documents; images; blogs; and newsgroups; not to mention a plethora of bibliographic sources, such as Web gateways and guides. Many of these Web resources are supported by volunteer efforts and are unstable, some require special software, and a number are at least partially fee-based.

Although it is hard to argue with users' preferences for the open Web, it is important to realize that the content available may be incomplete, of variable quality, and transient. Metadata is often either lacking or inconsistent, search results may be skewed by commercial factors, and texts are not structured in a way that makes them compatible with bibliographic management software. The pathway for research from discovery to full-text documents to writing and publication can be blocked at many points, leaving researchers frustrated at their inability to obtain or download documents they find on the Web. Traditional scholarly databases remain superior in their ability to describe, organize, and connect information in a consistent, structured way. However, if users restrict themselves to a single access tool, many will choose to limit their research to the free Web. Reference librarians try to combat this tendency through education. Does any other remedy exist?

Reference librarians have attempted to include free Web reference serials in virtual library collections by selectively listing them in the library catalog, in electronic database listings, and in research guides prepared by subject specialists. These efforts are all good in their way, but the necessity to search licensed library resources apart from the free Web remains a major inconvenience in the eyes of many library users. One possible solution is the Google Scholar model, in which scholarly societies and commercial reference publishers provide their bibliographic data to search engines.[17] The problem with this model is that if it becomes the norm, publishers might lose their source of revenue and cease publication, with disastrous results for scholarship.[18] If the search engine were to compensate reference publishers for their information, there is concern that this cost might eventually be passed on to users through obtrusive advertising or end-user fees. Another possible model would be that of open access reference databases funded not by subscription fees but by the cooperative, voluntary contributions of libraries, government, scholarly societies, and other institutions.[19]

It may appear to reference librarians that they have been left on the sidelines in some of these developments, but they underestimate their importance as advisers and partners with product developers and publishers. Reference librarians should continually examine the role played by reference sources of different types, and if they conclude that the regular, consistent, and accurate gathering, publication, and accumulation of factual and bibliographic information is important to scholarship, they should be prepared to support scholarly reference publishers in innovative ways. In the short term, continuing to work with publishers to establish and maintain fair pricing structures and innovations for improved access is essential. It is also crucial to frequently consult with faculty and graduate students at both the local and the national levels about their need for traditional subject databases, which may differ greatly across disciplines. The open access option should be pursued when appropriate, although this option seems more likely to succeed for disciplinary journals than for reference publishing, which requires greater coordination over a long period of time. Without the support of libraries, market forces may prematurely force trade publishers and scholarly societies out of the reference business with unknown consequences. If this happens, let it only be because better choices have evolved to serve the purposes of the erstwhile reference serial.

REFERENCE NOTES

1. Recent in-depth interviews of graduate students at CMU revealed that locating the full text of publications they had discovered in a published bibliography or through a Web search engine was a major challenge. Results of this survey will be published in 2006. Joan Stein et al., "In Their Own Words: A Preliminary Report on the Value of the Internet and the Library in Graduate Student Research," *Performance Measurement and Metrics* 7, no. 2 (2006): 107–15. The same phenomenon has also been reported by reference librarians. The Web increasingly provides citation lists, bibliographies, and course reading lists, which generate a host of challenging known-item searches.

2. Carol Tenopir, "Online Scholarly Journals: How Many?" *Library Journal* 129, no. 2 (1 February 2004): 32.

3. Dave Tyckoson, "Facts Go Online: Are Print Reference Collections Still Relevant?" *Against the Grain* 16, no. 4 (September 2004): 34–38; Walter Bell, "Is Print Reference Dead?" *ALA Cognotes* (Midwinter Meeting 2005, part 5): 4.

4. The five peer institutions were the California Institute of Technology, Emory University, the Massachusetts Institute of Technology, Rensselaer Polytechnic Institute, and Washington University in St. Louis. All analysis was done on the basis of publicly available data.

5. Library Statistics Program, "Compare Academic Libraries, 2002 data," Institute of Education Sciences, U.S. Department of Education, http://nces.ed.gov/surveys/libraries/compare/Academic.asp (accessed 13 December 2005).

6. At CMUL, a subject database in the common fund continues to be considered in some sense the property of the contributing department, and the department can make changes and substitutions on its own authority as long as there is no net change in cost.

7. See, for example, Stuart D. Lee, *Electronic Collection Development: A Practical Guide* (New York: Neal Schuman, 2002). Sample reference collection policies are available in *Reference Collection Development: A Manual*, ed. Alice J. Perez, RUSA Occasional Paper #27 (Chicago: RUSA, 2004).

8. A good selection of papers and bibliographies on this topic can be found at "From Text to Technology: The Changing Reference Collection," a 2002 CODES program, www.lib.utah.edu/genref/lkeiter/2002.html (accessed 13 December 2005). See also Ann Bristow, "Acquiring Reference Tools: Some Thoughts on Current Issues," *Acquisitions Librarian* 29 (2003): 13–22.

9. Based on an ongoing CMUL database of serials cancellation forms.

10. Deborah D. Blecic, Joan B. Fiscella, and Stephen E. Wiberley, "The Measurement of Use and Web-based Information Resources: An Early Look at Vendor-supplied Data," *College & Research Libraries* 62, no. 5 (September 2001): 434–53.

11. Lee, *Electronic Collection Development*, 62–97.

12. This discussion owes much to February 2004 interviews with Alice Bright, serials librarian; Denise Novak, head of acquisitions; and Kimberly Sestili, accounts manager at CMUL. For an overview of some longstanding, if not entirely current, issues, see *E-Serials Collection Management: Transitions, Trends, and Technicalities*, ed. David Fowler (New York: Haworth, 2004).

13. According to the CMU graduate student survey referred to above in note 1, this situation has changed little since the final report of the major British user study JUSTEIS in 2001, www.dil.aber.ac.UK/dils/Research/JUSTEIS (accessed 28 December 2005).

14. Library Landscape, "2003 Environmental Scan," www.oclc.org/membership/escan/library/default.htm (accessed 13 December 2005).

15. William Fisher, "Now You See It; Now You Don't: The Elusive Nature of Electronic Information," *Library Collections, Acquisitions, & Technical Services* 27 (2003): 463–72.

16. Marcus P. Zillman, "Academic and Scholar Search Engines and Sources." An Internet MiniGuide Annotated Link Compilation, http://VirtualPrivateLibrary.BlogSpot.com/Scholar.pdf (accessed 13 December 2005).

17. A description of the Google Scholar project can be found at http://scholar.google.com/intl/en/scholar/about.html (accessed 14 July 2006). For an empirical study comparing the content of Google Scholar with that of a number of research databases, see Chris Neuhaus, Ellen Neuhaus, and Alan Asher, "The Depth and Breadth of Google Scholar: An Empirical Study," *Portal* 6 (April 2006): 127-41.

18. At a meeting of book publishers, Bloomsbury cofounder Nigel Newton was quoted as saying, "We are being given an opportunity to undermine our industry. It may not seem inherently scary at the moment. But my concern is what this will lead to in 10 years. We are opening a Pandora's Box, and we have no idea where it will lead. We just don't know, once they have this material, what they will do with it." Philip Jones, "Bloomsbury Exec Warns Against Google Print," *The Book Standard* (April 20, 2005) www.thebookstandard.com/bookstandard/news/global/article_display.jsp?vnu_content_id=1000891650 (accessed 9 March 2007).

19. For a lucid analysis of the open access question from the point of view of a scholarly society and its funding needs, see Roy Rozenzweig, "Should Scholarly Publishing Be Free?" *Perspectives* 43 (April 2005): 11–15.

6 Electronic Resources in the Legal Research Environment

STEPHANIE SCHMITT

If it's legal, it's probably a serial.[1]

Most materials in a law library are serials or materials that behave like serials. Primary sources, such as laws, regulations, judgments, opinions, briefs, and reports are frequently published in parts and are constantly updated, revised, or replaced. Secondary sources, such as commentaries, analyses, and case books, are also regularly supplemented, updated, or replaced, so that even though they are described as monographs—which are referred to by law librarians as *treatises*—they are often treated as serials from a bibliographic standpoint.

"Legal periodical literature ranges from the theoretical essays and serious scholarship in academic law reviews to the practical 'how to do it' articles in bar journals."[2] There are four major types of legal periodicals: law reviews published by academic institutions, bar association publications, journals published by commercial publishers, and legal newspapers. The foundation of every major law collection, in addition to the primary sources, consists of academic law reviews, and providing access to that material has always been the number one priority of law libraries.

After a number of mergers and acquisitions, a handful of legal publishers now dominate the industry, creating a virtual monopoly on the publication of primary source material.[3] The largest legal publishers, Thomson, parent company of West Publishing Company and the Research Institute of America, and Reed Elsevier, which owns the LexisNexis group that includes Shepards and Matthew Bender, together with Wolters Kluwer, parent company of Aspen Publishing and Commerce Clearing House, account for 80 percent of all legal publications in the United States. They are experiencing growth of 3 to 4 percent a year and share profits of nearly $6 billion annually.[4]

While the large legal publishers are focused on producing primary source material and gaining the much coveted designation of official publisher of state statutes and legislative session laws, a number of major commercial publishers, including Springer, Blackwell, Elsevier, and Sage Publications control the marketplace for secondary source material and journals.[5] Association and society publications account for another segment of the market and are the source of much valuable information. However, the most unusual component in the legal publishing field—academic law reviews—gives legal publishing its unique flavor. Most law schools in North America sponsor at least one law review, and many law schools sponsor several. The journals generally have modest subscription rates and are often heavily subsidized by the parent institution. In most cases, the editorial board is composed entirely of students, and competition to serve on the board is usually intense. Students are responsible for all aspects of the editorial and production process, from solicitation and review of manuscripts to cite checking and editing to business management, including handling subscriptions and advertising. Academic law reviews differ from other law journals by virtue of the fact that they do not adhere to the peer-review process, the critical component of journal publishing in almost all other disciplines. Instead, students evaluate all submissions, even those from the most accomplished, prominent legal scholars.[6]

The Transition to Electronic Format

To support the diverse needs and interests of their users, law libraries, whether in firms or in academe, must take a multidisciplinary approach to collecting and providing access to a wide range of legal and nonlegal publications. Timely delivery and ease of access to information are the enduring measures of excellence for legal research services and the number one priority of law libraries. The electronic environment offers many opportunities for libraries to reaffirm that priority by allowing them to expand the scope and coverage of their collections. However, the subjects collected and the primary and secondary sources to which access is provided are determined by the focus of a firm's practice or reflected by the research needs of a law school's faculty, and depend not only on the mandate of the organization and the needs of the clientele being served but also on available resources.

By the mid-1950s, the power of electronic publishing had already been recognized. Lexis has its roots in software developments made at that time, and after many years of experimentation was finally introduced to the American legal community in 1973. It began modestly by offering full-text federal statutes and case law, federal tax information, and a selection of state documents. The first release of Westlaw, based on the West Publishing Company's unique system of headnotes took place in April 1975, but it was only after being completely redesigned in the early 1980s, that it offered any real competition to Lexis.[7] After more than two decades as the unrivaled leaders in providing online access to legal publications, the two databases are ubiquitous. The impact Lexis and Westlaw have had on legal research is enormous, and it is completely unthinkable to conduct legal research without these two giants of legal publishing.

The success and power of Lexis and Westlaw were certainly factors in setting the stage for other publishers, both in the profit and nonprofit sectors, to begin exploring the benefits and potential of the digital format for efficient and economical distribution of legal information. Those federal and state agencies under legislative mandates that require government information to be readily accessible to the public are committed to the production of documents in electronic form. Such powerful organizations as the American Bar Association as well as such specialized groups as the National Institute for Trial Advocacy are heavily invested in electronic publishing. Academic law reviews have been slower to accept electronic publishing as a viable alternative to traditional publishing, but they too are beginning to recognize and take advantage of the benefits of electronic access.

Although there is increasing interest from all spheres of legal publishing in utilizing electronic formats to their utmost potential, lawyers and legal scholars are faced with a major dilemma: The rules of legal citation, whether in a court of law or in a scholarly publication, often stipulate that the printed document should be considered as the authoritative source.

Despite the burgeoning number of electronic resources, the standard for legal citation continues to be the print version of a document. For several years, various groups, including the American Bar Association and the American Association of Law Libraries have actively lobbied the courts to "implement citation standards that are not keyed to print," but so far, this effort has been unsuccessful.[8] Consequently, *The Bluebook: A Uniform System of Citation,* labeled as "the definitive style guide for legal citation in the United States," continues to stipulate that the standard for legal citation is the print version of primary legal sources. Rule 18 "requires the use and citation of traditional printed sources unless (1) the information cited is unavailable in the traditional printed source; or (2) a copy of the source cannot be located because it is so obscure that it is practically unavailable. Only in these two cases should citation be made to the electronic source alone."[9] The impact of this situation on publishing, collection development, and research is significant.[10] Publishers are fully aware of this requirement and are striving not only to make their titles available in a format that is acceptable within the guidelines of legal citation but also to provide exact equivalents of their print publications in digital form. For example, the Government Printing Office (GPO) developed GPO Access, which provides federal government documents online as PDF files, and since 2002, Westlaw has made the contents of its National Reporter Series available in PDF format.[11]

In retrospect, it seems somewhat ironic that Lexis and Westlaw, the early pioneers of electronic access to legal literature, whose databases have become the staple of every law school and many law firm collections, provided electronic documents in a format that was not acceptable for citation purposes.[12] Fortunately, as electronic publishing and online access mature, legal publishers are beginning to produce electronic documents in formats that are compatible with the requirements of legal citation. These changes are encouraging from a management as well as an accessibility perspective and indicate a recognition and acceptance of the new online environment. In the final analysis, however, it is the courts that establish citation norms, and they "retain full editorial responsibility for citable, final and official versions of their opinions."[13]

Scholars as well as practicing attorneys have found that electronic access to the latest court decisions and to new legislation or changes to existing legislation satisfies their need for timely and efficient delivery of information. At the same time, law librarians have discovered that there are significant challenges inherent in managing a collection of electronic resources, and routine practices and procedures must be adjusted to meet these challenges. While publishers have been encouraged to create utilities that provide information directly to researchers, who are enthusiastic about using these tools, librarians run the risk of creating an environment that could lead to their obsolescence as a profession. Not only must librarians learn to maintain these new online collections but they must reinvent themselves as experts in managing digital formats to remain viable in the new environment. This effort will require that law librarians promulgate the growth of online collections and promote the transition to electronic versions of legal texts in the classroom, in research, in editing law reviews, and eventually, in the courts. Librarians will be successful if they embrace electronic formats, consider digital alternatives when making collection development decisions, and utilize all available resources to provide access to and encourage the use of electronic materials.

Supporting efficient and timely legal research is an expensive proposition and requires librarians to make difficult choices. In this regard, law libraries are struggling with the same issues as other libraries—coping with status quo budgets while trying to find ways to balance the users' desire for electronic resources with existing fiscal realities. As larger and larger portions of the budget are earmarked for the acquisition and maintenance of electronic resources, other collection development opportunities have to be modified or abandoned. Because the rules of citation continue to require that the authoritative version of a document be the printed version, many law libraries have been forced to maintain their print collections, resulting in an even greater strain on the library budget.

Although Lexis and Westlaw dominate the legal database scene, other legal publishers, such as the Bureau of National Affairs, have also entered the electronic arena.[14] These other publishers are aggressively marketing their electronic products to libraries. Unlike Westlaw and Lexis, who license databases *in toto*, many smaller publishers allow libraries to license electronic resources individually or in clusters. In some cases, publishers are simply creating digitized replicas of their print material; in other cases, publishers are digitizing selected parts or supplementing the printed version with material in digital form. In still other instances, publishers are eliminating print publications entirely in favor of online products. Some publishers have created digital content that differs from the publications' print relatives and functions more like databases or portals, linking to information both within the resource as well as to external resources, thus adding to their appeal as well as their value as research tools.

Whereas the large legal publishers may claim virtual monopolies on publishing primary sources, commentaries, and legal analysis, for the most part, they have not ventured into journal publishing, preferring to leave that to the commercial publishers. Journal publication is undergoing a major transformation as publishers seek effective business strategies that will allow them to maintain market share as well as fiscal viability. Site licenses on a title-by-title basis and a variety of package deals based on broad topics are among the attractive options law libraries must consider. In addition, publishers, librarians, and scholars alike are keeping an eye on new publishers, such as Berkeley Electronic Press (bepress), who are experimenting with new distribution models based solely on electronic publication.[15]

Academic law reviews, central to the law school experience, are relative latecomers to online publication. Their belated entry into the online environment centered on the need to adhere to the rules governing legal citation. In 2000, a bold venture by the William S. Hein & Company ushered in a new era with the launch of HeinOnline.[16] Initially conceived to provide comprehensive full-text coverage from the inception of each academic law review, the database now includes fully searchable, full-text PDF files of more than eight hundred journals, all U.S. treaties and agreements, and every published U.S. Supreme Court decision as it appears in the *U.S. Reports.*[17] In addition to the breadth of its coverage, HeinOnline is valuable for scholars because the PDF format makes the online documents acceptable for citation purposes. The database is also significant for law libraries because it offers subscribing institutions a viable option about the disposition of their print collections, certain in the knowledge that they can provide access to documents that meet the requirements of legal citation.

The looseleaf format has been a staple of legal publishing for many years. It is cost-effective in terms of production, lends itself to rapid updating, and is preferred by researchers because of its currency. Publishers are aware that making looseleaf publications electronically accessible not only provides an excellent alternative to the traditional looseleaf format but is also a bonus for the legal researcher. In electronic format, the content is often updated more frequently than in the print counterpart, and the online version almost always offers greater flexibility in terms of searching capabilities and the speed with which information can be retrieved. Additionally, as libraries license access to the material online, the amount of physical processing and collection maintenance of the looseleaf collection is reduced.

Following the trend toward electronic publishing, the federal government is also rapidly moving into the electronic arena.[18] Through GPO Access, the GPO is fully committed to making federal government publications available online, and government agencies are equally committed to this goal. Similar projects are taking place at the state and local level, so the amount of material that is readily accessible is growing at an amazing rate.

The increase in the amount of legal material available online extends well beyond domestic publications. Foreign and international materials are also becoming more readily accessible electronically. Primary source materials, such as official United Nations publications, are accessible through Lexis and Westlaw, as well as directly from the United Nations Web site. Other multinational organizations, such as the Council of Europe, maintain their own Web sites; however, the amount of historical material is still somewhat scarce. Of the thousands of nongovernmental organizations (NGOs), only a small fraction has adopted the concept of online publishing, although the numbers are growing as NGOs discover the usefulness of a strong Web presence to support their work.

The countries of Western Europe are at the forefront of the online movement. However, countries in what is generally considered the developing world have been quick to discover that electronic publishing provides greater benefits than more traditional forms of publishing, although access to legal information in these countries depends in large measure on the availability of Web access. Reports from the Pew Global Attitudes Project and the World Intellectual Property Organization explore the ongoing patterns of growth in Internet use throughout the world.[19] Although progress is not uniform, "the countries that have experienced most digital development include those that have placed emphasis on e-government."[20]

Selecting and Managing Electronic Resources

Selecting and acquiring electronic resources in the law library environment is based on many of the same criteria used by libraries in general and is usually done in response to the needs of the library's constituents. The process typically begins with an evaluation of the content, functionality, and overall usability of the resource and a search for answers to the following questions:

- Does the title meet the needs of the user community?
- What acquisitions arrangements are available?
- Are there access or use restrictions that must be considered?
- Is the title available through a package or a group purchase?

When electronic resources were still a novelty, publishers often made the online version of a publication available at no additional cost, provided the library maintained its print subscription. With the growing popularity of electronic materials, publishers have been experimenting with a variety of subscription models all designed to give them greater exposure while still maintaining fiscal viability. In some cases, access to the online version is available for an additional fee over and above the cost of the print subscription, or, alternatively, the print subscription is available for a surcharge to the online price. Taking advantage of cooperative purchasing arrangements with established consortia, such as the New England Law Library Consortium, or through collaboration with other groups of libraries may also be advantageous for law libraries, and offers libraries opportunities to enhance collections at affordable prices beyond what they could negotiate independently.[21]

Law libraries, like other such institutions, face significant challenges and workflow adjustments as they shift from primarily print-based collections to collections largely comprised of electronic resources. When procedural and policy changes are needed to support collections of electronic resources and changes to bibliographic description are discussed in order to improve access to the resources, sufficient time should be set aside to consider the impact of these changes both on the staff and on the researcher. The introduction of new tools of discovery, such as A–Z lists and link resolvers, will not only greatly expand the number of access points but may also be accompanied by technical challenges that require significant investments of time, money, and training.

Conclusion

Managing electronic resources requires constant maintenance and assessment. Does the library's catalog reflect what is available to the legal community? Are the resources being used and by whom? Evaluation tools, such as user surveys, and statistical information, such as usage statistics, are crucial if the library is to make well-informed judgments about the impact and value of electronic resources as part of the collection.

The law library's strength is derived from a combination of collections and services. The typical law library acquires and supports a variety of electronic resources, but if selection criteria, staffing, and support requirements are not adequately addressed, the strong service orientation may languish. The transition toward the electronic environment should be measured through evaluative usage studies and balanced with a thorough understanding of the methods, requirements, and habits of the institution's legal researchers. The number of electronic resources devoted to law and managed by a law library is quite small. Nevertheless, the issues law librarians must deal with are very similar to those of their counterparts in larger organizations. In addition, the broad interests of legal researchers and scholars suggest the need to expand opportunities for online access.

Law libraries must find ways to accommodate the changes necessary to successfully integrate electronic collections with print collections. More importantly, the transition from a print-based collection to one that is heavily weighted toward electronic resources should be done in a way that facilitates research and encourages widespread participation in the new environment. It also is important to keep in mind that over time there will be changes in the way legal research is conducted, and the arbiters of legal citation will adapt to those changes. In the future, perhaps sooner than anticipated, digitized resources, regardless of form, will be recognized and as acceptable as print resources. Publishers and database providers are already improving their products and enhancing the granularity of the reference points within articles. For example, plans for digital object identifiers include the ability to identify and cite a graphic or table within an article.[22] Digital journals could routinely provide line numbers or identifiable quadrants within sections of articles to aid citation consistency, the greatest concern of citation verification. This suggestion is one among hundreds that seek to ease the print-bias embedded in the requirements of current legal research. The options are as numerous as the law librarians who endeavor to support digital legal collections, and solutions are around the corner for some of the concerns with which the legal research community currently grapples.

REFERENCE NOTES

1. Janet McKinney, "If It's Legal, It's Probably a Serial," *Serials Librarian* 38, no. 3-4 (2000): 299–303.

2. Morris L. Cohen, Robert C. Berring, and Kent C. Olson, *How to Find the Law*, 9th ed. (St. Paul: West Publishing, 1989), 359.

3. Mary H. Munroe, "The Academic Publishing Industry: A Story of Merger and Acquisition," Northern Illinois University Libraries, www.niulib.niu.edu/publishers (accessed 22 May 2006).

4. Kendall F. Svengalis, "The Current State of the Legal Publishing Industry and Its Implications for Law Libraries," Rhode Island Law Press, 2002, www/rilawpress .com/orall_presentation.ppt (accessed 18 July 2006).

5. LexisNexis Media Relations, "LexisNexis Named Publisher of Official Reports by California Supreme Court," LexisNexis Press Center, 18 April 2003. Abstract can be viewed and article purchased at http://goliath.ecnext.com/coms2/gi_0199-2693951/ LexisNexis-Named-Publisher-of-Official.html (accessed 29 May 2006). States have become savvy to the concept and have learned to include beneficial terms in contracts with publishers. For example, the Supreme Court of California negotiated with LexisNexis to be the publishers of their official reports. The contract with LexisNexis included "free access to the official text [to anyone in the State of California] of the opinions at a Website hosted by LexisNexis linked to the courts Website."

6. For a detailed description of the history of law reviews, see Bernard J. Hibbitts, "Last Writes: Re-assessing the Law Review in the Age of Cyberspace," University of Pittsburgh Law School, www.law.pitt.edu/hibbitts/lw_p1.htm (accessed 29 May 2006).

7. A headnote is a summary that is prepared by a West Publishing Company editor about a point of law found in a court opinion. Headnotes are added to the opinion and are part of the annotations (or value added) by West Publishing Company to official case reports. See also Hibbitts, "Last Writes."

8. Peter W. Martin, "Who Sets Citation Norms," *Introduction to Basic Legal Citation.* § 1-600, www.law.cornell.edu/citation/1-600.htm (accessed 30 May 2006).

9. *The Bluebook: A Uniform System of Citation*, 18th ed. (Cambridge, Mass.: Harvard Law Review, 2005), 3.

10. Although some state courts, such as New York and California, have their own citation rules, the *Bluebook* remains the standard for citing legal information. Another citation manual that is quite widely used is the Association of Legal Writing Directors and Darby Dickerson, *ALWD Citation Manual: A Professional System of Citation*, 3d ed. (New York: Aspen, 2006).

11. GPO Access (www.gpoaccess.gov/index.html) is a free service of the United States Government Printing Office that provides electronic access to the official, published

version of material issued by the federal government. The service is funded by the Federal Depository Library Program and was established by Public Law 103-40, the Government Printing Office Electronic Information Enhancement Act of 1993.

12. To be fair, when Lexis and Westlaw first began providing content electronically, the technology to produce exact replicas of printed documents did not exist.

13. Martin, "Who Sets Citation Norms."

14. The Bureau of National Affairs has developed a number of databases that complement their printed and electronic publications. For details, see www.bna.com/ (accessed 29 May 2006).

15. Berkeley Electronic Press, www.bepress.com/ (accessed 29 May 2006).

16. William S. Hein and Company, www.wshein.com/ (accessed 29 May 2006).

17. The official reporter of the Supreme Court is known as the *United States Reports*, www.supremecourtus.gov/opinions/boundvolumes.html (accessed 24 July 2006). "Only the printed bound volumes of the United States Reports contain the final, official opinions of the Supreme Court of the United States."

18. For information on the growth of online resource and the use of those resources by the general public, see John B. Horrigan's *How Americans Get in Touch with Government*, Pew Internet & American Life Project, Washington, D.C., 2004, www .pewinternet.org/pdfs/PIP_E-Gov_Report_0504.pdf (accessed 9 June 2006).

19. Andrew Kohut, "Truly a World Wide Web: Globe Going Digital," 2005 Pew Global Attitudes Survey, Washington, D.C., 2006, http://pewglobal.org/reports/pdf/251.pdf (accessed 15 July 2006).

20. World Intellectual Property Organization, *Intellectual Property on the Internet: A Survey of Issues* (Geneva: WIPO, 2002), 148, www.wipo.int/copyright/ecommerce/en/ pdf/survey.pdf (accessed 15 July 2006).

21. New England Law Library Consortium, www.nellco.org/ (accessed 29 May 2006).

22. Digital Object Identifier System, www.doi.org/ (accessed 29 May 2006).

7 Serials Management in an Academic Health Sciences Library

ROBIN KLEIN, PATRICIA HINEGARDNER,
ALEXA MAYO, AND JANE MURRAY

Distinguished as the first library established by a medical school in the United States, the Health Sciences and Human Services Library (HS/ HSL) at the University of Maryland provides resources and services for more than eleven thousand faculty, staff, and students in the schools of nursing, medicine, dentistry, pharmacy, and social work and for an inter-disciplinary graduate school. The HS/HSL is the only publicly supported health sciences library in Maryland. Sixty-five full-time equivalent staff, including twenty-five faculty librarians, staff the library.

The library also supports the University of Maryland Medical Center (UMMC), a 648-bed academic medical center that trains more than half of Maryland's physicians and other health-care professionals. The medical center cares for more than thirty thousand inpatients and two hundred thousand outpatients each year, and has many world-renowned special-ized programs. Clinical staff members from UMMC, as well as consumers using the medical center's facilities, draw upon the services and collections of HS/HSL.

In addition, as one of eight contractual regional medical libraries (RML) in the National Library of Medicine's National Network of Libraries of Medicine, HS/HSL serves physicians and consumers throughout the South-eastern/Atlantic region. As the RML, the library's mission is to provide "all U.S. health professionals with equal access to biomedical information provide the general public in the region with information through docu-ment delivery and reference services to make informed decisions about their health."[1] Serving as the RML provides opportunities for the library staff to observe health-care professionals in a variety of settings and leads to an understanding of the health information needs of the region.

92

Clientele

The library serves a diverse clientele, including health-care practitioners, basic science researchers, clinical instructors, students, and the general public. Information needs vary from physicians searching for in-depth clinical information to members of the general public seeking health information for themselves or family members, and the information provided must be current, accurate, easily available, and rapidly delivered to the inquirer.

Selection

The library maintains a strong collection of resources to support education, research, and clinical practice through an active collection development program. Subscriptions to print and electronic, or e-journal, collections are handled through direct subscriptions with publishers and vendors and participation in consortial agreements with Maryland hospital libraries, the sixteen-library University System of Maryland and Affiliated Institutions (USMAI), and with the state wide consortium of academic libraries, Maryland Digital Library. Some of these arrangements provide HS/HSL with aggregated packages from which titles within scope are selected and added to the library's e-journal list. Some packages contain embargoed titles that create barriers to obtaining current health information.

Selection is made using available core lists, such as *Doody's Core Titles in the Health Sciences,* and until ceasing publication in 2003, the periodically issued *Brandon/Hill Selected Lists.*[2] A challenge to effectively selecting materials for a broad health sciences collection is the lack of core lists in such interdisciplinary areas as social work, requiring librarians to create their own methods to evaluate collections in those areas.[3]

Faculty, staff, students, and faculty librarians with subject expertise recommend titles to purchase and the collection development department maintains a desiderata list, tracking price, online availability, and adherence to scope, according to HS/HSL collection development guidelines.[4] Journal requests are reviewed and information about the requestor is shared with faculty librarians, who review the recommendations for indexing, regional availability (i.e., availability at other USMAI campuses), and impact factor.

The library's journal review committee and the digital resources committee evaluate the suggestions for print and electronic titles respectively. The committees refer to the digital resources collection development policy to make their recommendations, and final purchasing decisions are made in conjunction with the library director.[5] The disproportionate rise in the prices of science, technology, and medical (STM) journal titles, coupled with local budgetary constraints during the past five years, have pushed cancellation projects to prominence, and purchasing decisions are not made lightly. The cancellation projects have evolved into an annual analysis of the journal collection, in which both cost and title cost-per-use, extrapolated from in-house use (derived from a quarterly sampling of reshelving statistics, because journals do not circulate) and online use statistics, impact factor, online availability, interlibrary loan (ILL) use, and other variables are considered.

Input from the campus community is regularly solicited through a heavily publicized online survey that typically is mounted on the library's Web site for several weeks in the spring. A library advisory committee, comprised of faculty librarians and student and faculty representatives from each of the schools, provides input on collection decisions and encourages participation in the survey.

Ongoing review of the collection is important, as is communicating with users about potential journal cuts. Constituents are informed of purchase and cancellation decisions through several media, including e-mail announcements sent by library advisory committee members, articles on the library's Web site, and notices in the in-house newsletter, *HS/HSL unplugged*.[6] Faculty librarians, in conjunction with an active library liaison program, directly communicate collection changes to faculty in the specific areas of subject expertise.

In keeping with the public health aspects of the HS/HSL's mission, the need for both current health information and access to historical material must be factored into the selection process. It is also important to consider the perils of publishers' embargoes for titles of clinical significance. Healthcare professionals must have access to the latest treatment information to make informed decisions on patient care. When selecting titles for the collection, the library considers the following issues:

> STM journals are among the most expensive in publishing;
>
> pricing and accessibility varies based on whether a title is offered in a print and online combination or only as a print or online subscription;
>
> access to subscribed content must be retained, even if an online subscription is cancelled, and ongoing costs, if any, to maintain access to that content must be considered; and
>
> some vendors and publishers assess site license fees in addition to subscription costs that must be analyzed and figured in as part of the annual subscription fees.

With these considerations in mind, it is necessary to adopt creative strategies to work within the constraints of a flat budget. One strategy is to

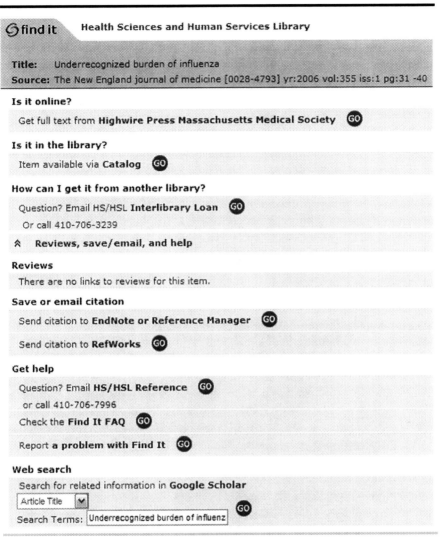

FIGURE 1
"Find It" NEJM

Management and Presentation

Like many other libraries, HS/HSL maintains some electronic resource metadata in its online catalog as well as in a Web-based A–Z list.[9] HS/HSL shares a catalog with the other USMAI libraries, and consortium policies dictate how and which electronic resource titles are represented in the shared catalog. When possible within these policy constraints, e-journals are cataloged and added to the library's OPAC.

From the late 1990s until 2005, the HS/HSL's e-journals were represented in a locally developed A–Z list and the specialized interests of the library's user community drove decision making about which online journals were presented in that list. Aggregated packages, such as EBSCO's Academic Search Premier, were reviewed for specific in-scope titles that could be hyperlinked and listed in the A–Z list. Although the list was arranged alphabetically and could be searched by title, users could also limit their searches by provider.

Maintenance of a local A–Z list is a time-consuming process. Titles are added and dropped by aggregators; titles and URLs change, often without prior notification. The need to control the front-end display with some back-end management functionality has spawned the development of public access management services (PAMS), such as Serial Solutions and TDNet. Through established relationships with publishers, these vendors handle the time-consuming tasks of tracking journal management information on behalf of libraries. HS/HSL staff recognized that such an arrangement guaranteed the accuracy of holdings displays and also offered significant timesavings, and in 2005, HS/HSL entered into an agreement with Serials Solutions to maintain its online journal A–Z list. Technical services staff are adding print information to the list to give users a complete picture of the library's journal holdings. Much behind-the-scenes work is still necessary to create an accurate profile of the library's subscriptions, but the result is a standardized, enhanced list of titles with good search functionality and subject category assignments. When the Serials Solutions A–Z list was introduced, the number of titles tracked increased fivefold from the original holdings information, to include peripheral titles from consortium-licensed databases, such as Academic Search Premier and JSTOR, as well as free aggregators, such as the Directory of Open Access Journals, which the HS/HSL uses.[10]

In 2003, when the HS/HSL prepared a new request for proposal (RFP) for the acquisition of subscription services, criteria were added to the technical specifications that delineated the online journal management services the library was interested in obtaining. These services included the capability to troubleshoot access problems, a crucial and time-consuming activity that is part of the management process for vendor and librarian alike. HS/HSL staff designed an in-house database for library staff that contains basic administrative data about resources, including interlibrary loan permissions, but maintenance of this database has not eliminated the library's need for a more comprehensive online mechanism to handle such tasks as monitoring trials and reviewing licenses. A more robust electronic resource management system that integrates publisher and library data would be a welcome addition to the library's suite of management tools.

One small but critical aspect of managing a collection of health sciences serials is the development of a mechanism to identify articles that have been retracted. HS/HSL technical services staff handles retractions. Searching the Medline database using an auto alert service, staff identifies the retracted articles, locates them in the physical journals, and stamps them as retracted. Online articles are similarly tagged and are searchable by PubMed and many other databases. It is especially important to tag retracted articles in health-related literature because incorrect information may adversely affect the health of a patient.

Staffing

The selection, accession, cataloging, management, and maintenance of electronic resources have increased not only the complexity of serials management but also the complexity of the relationships among staff. Fortunately, HS/HSL has a long history of highly successful cross-functional teams, and the flexibility of these work groups served the library well as staff adjusted to new needs and workflows. At HS/HSL, collection development for print and electronic resources is coordinated between public and technical services librarians. The digital resources committee, which reviews and evaluates requests for electronic resources, is composed of a cross-section of librarians from public services, technical services, and administration. In 2000, it became obvious that one position could no longer juggle responsibilities both for print and electronic resources, and as a result, a digital resources librarian position was created to oversee the acquisition and management of electronic resources. Although this position is part of the technical services team, the work requires considerable interaction with staff from a number of other departments, including information technology, reference, interlibrary loan, reserve, and cataloging on a regular basis.

At HS/HSL, detailed checklists track e-journals processing. Flowcharts and other troubleshooting tools help to manage the intersection between technical access problems that should be fielded by information technology staff and those more appropriately resolved by librarians. As subscriptions were converted from print to electronic formats, check-in and binding activities decreased, freeing staff to assume new responsibilities with the increasingly cumbersome management of e-journals. The introduction of electronic data interchange for invoicing relieved one staff member of the tedious task of manual invoice reconciliation. The transition from print to online serials has affected activities in other parts of the library as well—for example, shelvers spend less time reshelving journals—and redeployment of staff has become a wider issue than solely for those handling serials.

Conclusion

The library's goal when managing serials is to provide easy access to print and e-journals in an appropriate format at a reasonable cost for the library. There are many constants in the management of serials in any library, such as the importance of gathering usage statistics so that informed decisions about purchases and cancellations can be made, negotiating licenses that offer the most bang for the buck, dealing with the phenomenal rise in subscription costs for STM journals, and considering the use of online articles for document delivery and electronic reserve.

Libraries that support health information needs in a clinical setting face the additional challenge of providing up-to-date access to current information, while at the same time guaranteeing that access to archival information is readily accessible. The consequences of not providing adequate and timely health information to researchers and clinicians can have a significant impact on the health of an individual.

REFERENCE NOTES

1. The National Network of Libraries of Medicine's Southeastern/Atlantic Region includes Alabama, the District of Columbia, Florida, Georgia, Maryland, Mississippi, North Carolina, Puerto Rico, South Carolina, Tennessee, Virginia, West Virginia, and the U.S. Virgin Islands, http://nnlm.gov/sea/about/index.html (accessed 13 December 2005). For information about the Health Sciences and Human Services Library's contractual obligations as a member of the National Network of Libraries of Medicine, Southeastern/Atlantic Region, see www.hshsl.umaryland.edu/nnlm.html (accessed 10 April 2007).
2. *Doody's Core Titles in the Health Sciences* (Chicago: Doody Enterprises, 2004), www.doody.com/dct (accessed 28 December 2005); Dorothy R. Hill, Henry N. Stickell, and Suzanne J. Crow, "Brandon/Hill Selected List of Print Books and Journals for the Small Medical Library," 20th ed., Gustave L. and Janet W. Levy Library, Mount Sinai School of Medicine of New York University, New York, www.mssm.edu/library/brandon-hill/small_medical/pdf/brandon4.pdf (accessed 28 December 2005); Dorothy R. Hill and Henry N. Stickell, "Brandon/Hill Selected List of Print Books and Journals in Allied Health," *Journal of the Medical Library*

Association 91, no. 1 (2003): 18–33; Dorothy R. Hill and Henry N. Stickell, "Brandon/Hill Selected List of Print Nursing Books and Journals," *Nursing Outlook* 50, no. 3 (2003): 100–13.

3. Beth E. Jacoby et al., "Resource Selection for an Interdisciplinary Field: A Methodology," *Journal of the Medical Library Association* 90, no. 4 (2002): 393–99.

4. University of Maryland Health Sciences and Human Services Library, "Collection Development Policy, 10 August 1999," www.hshsl.umaryland.edu/information/colldev.html (accessed 21 July 2006).

5. University of Maryland Health Sciences and Human Services Library, "Digital Resources Collection Policy, 10 August 1999," rev. 12 April 2002, www.hshsl .hshsl.umaryland.edu/information/elecdev.html (accessed 25 July 2006).

6. *HS/HSL unplugged*, www.hshsl.umaryland.edu/information/news/unplugged.html (accessed 25 July 2006).

7. Peter Boyce et al., "How Electronic Journals Are Changing Patterns of Use," *Serials Librarian* 46, no. 1–2, (2004): 121.

8. Faith McLellan, "1966 and All That—When Is a Literature Search Done?" *Lancet* 358, no. 9282 (2001): 646.

9. Xiaotian Chen et al., "E-Resource Cataloging Practices: A Survey of Academic Libraries and Consortia," *Serials Librarian* 47, no. 1–2 (2004): 153.

10. Directory of Open Access Journals, www.doaj.org/ (accessed 25 July 2006).

Glossary

aggregator. A publisher who provides electronic access to multiple journal titles, all of which are published by that publisher; or a database that includes journals produced by one or several publishers. A publisher may have titles in one or several databases, but in both cases, the databases that bring together all the titles are called aggregator databases.

Ariel. A software product used to securely transmit documents electronically for interlibrary lending that controls the number of times authenticated users can view the document after it has been transmitted. License agreements often state that electronic transmission of a journal article is allowed through Ariel technology. Odyssey is another such product.

authentication. The process whereby a user is recognized as having the right to view online content is known as authentication. In many instances the user's IP (Internet Protocol) address is the method of recognition. As part of the establishment of an institutional online subscription, the subscriber provides the institution's IP addresses to the publisher. Users may also be authenticated by entering a username and password to a proxy server.

A–Z list. An alphabetical list of electronic journal titles that serve as hyperlinks to the journals' Web sites. This list is an efficient way to browse the journal titles available at a library. The list may also include the titles of online databases.

backfiles. Past or noncurrent issues of a journal, also known as *backruns*. Backfiles are made available to libraries in various ways, depending on the publisher and the extent to which a given title has been digitized.

Some publishers will sell a library the complete or partial backfiles of a journal, while other publishers will provide backfiles as part of a current subscription, and still others will provide their backfiles to an aggregator for sale to libraries as part of a package (JSTOR is an example of an aggregator of journal backfiles). Some subscriptions to current content may come with one year added *or* with one year dropped and one year added for each subscription year.

BIBCO. See *Monographic Bibliographic Record Program.*

big deal. A multiyear license agreement to all or a substantial portion of a publisher's catalog of titles. These arrangements are usually attractive because they save institutions money by locking in annual price increases and because they may provide access to titles that are not otherwise part of an institution's collection. Libraries belonging to consortia often find arrangements of this nature attractive. When a library enters into a predetermined financial commitment, cancellation before the end of the contract period may result in substantial penalties.

bundling. A collection of serial titles that must be obtained as a group, but may grant the subscriber the option of choosing print, print and online, or online-only formats, or a title supplied in both print and online formats as a package.

clustering. Software is available to organize results from a search query so that a searcher may more easily sort through categories of results. This organization of data for grouped display is called clustering.

Controlled LOCKSS (CLOCKSS). A partnership of publishers, libraries, and OCLC that provides a long-term archive of electronic journal content. This initiative builds on the efforts of LOCKSS to store the digital content of journals. CLOCKSS is a *dark* archive, which means that the contents are protected and intended to be used only if they are no longer available through other distribution means.

Cooperative Online Serials Program (CONSER). A component of the Program for Cooperative Cataloging (PCC) that is part of an international cooperative serials cataloging initiative to provide a source of high-quality bibliographic records for serials (see www.loc.gov/acq/conser/about .html).

digital object identifier. A unique and persistent naming convention for digital files or objects that form discreet groupings of information, images, or media on the Internet.

e-Depot. Developed in close cooperation between IBM and the National Library of the Netherlands, this software, in operation since 2003, harvests the online content of participating publishers and is structured to facilitate the transition to newer software, so that a viable permanent archive is maintained.

electronic resource management system (ERMS). Software used to manage electronic resources. A number of companies have developed ERMS based on the functional requirements established by the Digital Library Federation (DLF) (see www.diglib.org [accessed 16 March 2007]).

embargo. A publisher-imposed block on access to the most current content of electronic journals when these journals are part of an aggregated database. To receive current content, libraries must subscribe to the individual journals through a direct subscription. The time frame of the blocked material varies, but it is most commonly between six months to two years. As newer content is published, access to older content becomes available. This is referred to as a *moving wall*.

emulating software. Software that acts on electronic data in the same way as the original software used to create or maintain it, and thereby *emulates* the original software. Computer programs are software that usually changes over time with updates and new versions that can upgrade and add new functionality. Electronic journals, databases, and other electronic content use software to make them readable and useable. As software changes and content is stored in an electronic archive, there is concern about the usability of this content, and emulating software is one solution to this problem.

e-printers. The electronic counterpart of a traditional printer, e-printers take the electronic content of a third party and publish and distribute it from their servers over the Internet.

federated search. A search that simultaneously queries multiple databases and retrieves multiple or combined search results.

Google Scholar (http://scholar.google.com/, accessed 16 March 2007). A web search engine that harvests scholarly material in a great many disciplines and in a variety of publishing formats. Proprietary software that indexes peer-reviewed online journals with the exception of those published by Elsevier, who sells the competing Elsevier Scirus search product.

hosted. Electronic content that is licensed to one party but is stored and distributed on another party's server for access by authorized users. An example of hosting is when institutions that are independent of publishers make a mutual agreement to store and distribute electronic content in support of archiving the content, as in the case of LOCKSS.

impact factor. A measurement of the number of times an article is cited within a given time period. The impact factor divides the number of times an article is cited by the number of articles published during the preceding two years. This method helps to avoid a skewed comparison of journals of unequal size, frequency, and longevity. The impact factor is a tool for helping to determine the importance of a journal in a subject field.

infrastructure. The underlying structure that is necessary for a system to work. The system may be a building, a city, or a network that handles electronic content. The infrastructure for electronic journals is the server that stores and distributes the data, the network of wires and wireless communications for the dissemination of the data, and the receiver's or end-user's computing hardware that facilitates the download and storage of the data for reading and research.

Internet protocol (IP). The electronic address for an individual computer or server connected to the Internet. A range of IP addresses may represent a building or an institution. Often publishers will allow access to proprietary databases based on the IP addresses registered with them by the subscriber or subscribing institution. The IP address serves to authenticate the user as having the right to access the database.

leased content. Online journal and database content is most often not owned by the subscriber, but rather supplied by the publisher or provider of the information through subscription or ongoing annual fees.

legacy software. Software that is currently in use but may not be easily transferred to upgraded or different computing hardware.

license. A legal agreement or contract in which one party grants access to online journal and database content to another party or user. The license typically stipulates the provider's rights and responsibilities, the contractual and financial terms, and the procedures for resolution of breach of contract.

link resolver. A software protocol that helps the user navigate from a citation in an online index or catalog to the electronically available journal articles and chapters of books. This process is said to resolve the link between the two points, thus *link resolver*.

LOCKSS. See *Lots of Copies Keep Stuff Safe*.

looseleaf. Printed publication that is updated by inserting or interleafing new or revised printed content is called a looseleaf publication. The publication is often housed in a binder that allows for easy removal of outdated content and insertion of new and revised content. This type of publication is frequently used for legal and statutory materials.

Lots of Copies Keeps Stuff Safe (LOCKSS). Open source software developed by Stanford University that enables participating libraries to manage the digital content they have acquired. Copies of the content are stored digitally by several participating library members, allowing members to communicate with each other and safeguarding the content.

Monographic Bibliographic Record Program (BIBCO). Part of the Program for Cooperative Cataloging (PCC) at the Library of Congress. Libraries in this program contribute bibliographic records to a national bibliographic utility with full authority work, a national-level call number, and at least one subject heading from a nationally accepted subject list.

moving wall. See *embargo*.

NACO. See *Name Authority Cooperative Program*.

Name Authority Cooperative Program (NACO). Part of the Program for Cooperative Cataloging (PCC) at the Library of Congress. Libraries in this program follow standards to formulate name headings that are contributed to a nationally shared authority file.

online provider. A publisher or distributor of electronic content. The provider may be the publisher of the content or may host the content for distribution on behalf of a third party. Electronic journals and databases are available to users through online providers.

open access. Journal content that is available to users without charge. The cost of the publication is supported by the authors of the articles, the authors' institutions, or organizations that provide financial support for the work.

open source software. Computer programs that are freely available and have source code which can be modified to meet local needs. Open source code is promoted by the Open Source Initiative (www.opensource.org).

open URL. A software protocol that enables a URL to navigate the path from an online citation link to the online article. The URL usually captures the journal's ISSN, the issue number and date, the article's beginning page number, and sometimes the author and title data.

Portico. An electronic archiving service, supported by The Andrew W. Mellon Foundation, Ithaka, the Library of Congress, and JSTOR, that grew out of JSTOR's Electronic-Archiving Initiative in 2002. In 2004 the initiative became part of Ithaka Harbors, and Portico. Support for Portico was received from The Andrew W. Mellon Foundation, Ithaka, the Library of Congress, and JSTOR. Portico was launched in 2005. Publishers and libraries can participate in the archive as subscribing members. The digital files store journal content submitted by publishers in a format that can be easily migrated to new software in the future. The archive is designed as a repository of content to be used only when it can no longer be supplied by the publisher.

proxy server. Users who attempt to logon to proprietary databases must be authenticated as legitimate subscribers. This authentication can be accomplished by software which routes the user's request to a server, known as the proxy server. Once the user is authenticated, access to the electronic resource is established. Proxy servers are used to enable legitimate patrons to access electronic resources from outside a valid IP range. Proxy service is not necessary in cases where a password and ID are used to access a database.

repositories. A location where printed and electronic content is gathered and stored for safekeeping. A repository can be a building that houses such physical items as bound journal volumes and monographs, or a computer server that stores such digital content as text, images, and media.

request for proposal (RFP). A document that outlines the service and programmatic needs and expectations of an institution and invites technical and financial responses to satisfy those needs. RFPs are typically sent to several potential respondents in order to obtain multiple, competitive offers. Instead of an RFP, some organizations may issue a request for quotations (RFQ) or a request for information (RFI).

rich site summary (RSS). An electronic document feed that retrieves and delivers up-to-date Web content that is viewable on a computer through special software. RSS feeds are often used to provide updates from news providers and blogs. Also known as *Really Simple Syndication.*

SCCTP. See *Serials Cataloging Cooperative Training Program.*

selective dissemination of information (SDI). An alerting service that notifies individuals of new information based on the characteristics of a distinct profile. The content can be citations that are links to articles, a journal's tables of contents, or the routing of a journal or photocopied article.

serial. A publication that is intended to be ongoing and has enumeration or chronology to distinguish the periodic, annual, or irregular publication of issues. The term *serial* has been subsumed by the phrase *continuing resource*, which encompasses serials and integrating resources.

Serials Cataloging Cooperative Training Program (SCCTP). Program that provides materials and training to trainers who give standardized instruction for cataloging continuing resources.

subscription agent. A company that orders and processes serial titles on behalf of publishers.

surcharge. An additional fee levied by publishers for access to the electronic version of a journal that is available in both print and online. This additional fee is a percentage of the print cost and normally ranges between 5 and 25 percent. With the growing popularity of the online format, some publishers now levy a surcharge to receive the print version.

Contributors

Jean M. Alexander
 Head, Hunt Library Reference
 Carnegie Mellon University
 Pittsburgh, Pa.
 jeana@andrew.cmu.edu

John P. Blosser
 Head, Serials Department &
  Coordinator of Acquisitions
  Services
 Northwestern University Library
 Evanston, Ill.
 jblosser@northwestern.edu

Susan Davis
 Head, Electronic Periodicals
  Management Department
 Central Technical Services
 University at Buffalo (SUNY)
 Buffalo, N.Y.
 unlsdb@buffalo.edu

Cindy Hepfer
 Head, Electronic Periodicals
  Management Department
 Central Technical Services
 University at Buffalo (SUNY)
 Buffalo, N.Y.
 HSLcindy@buffalo.edu

Patricia Hinegardner
 Web Services Librarian
 Health Sciences and Human
  Services Library
 University of Maryland, Baltimore
 Baltimore, Md.
 phinegar@hshsl.umaryland.edu

Robin Klein
 Digital Resources Librarian
 Health Sciences and Human
  Services Library
 University of Maryland, Baltimore
 Baltimore, Md.
 rklein@hshsl.umaryland.edu

Harriet Lightman
 Bibliographer for History,
  Economics, French & Italian
  Literatures & Philosophy
 Northwestern University Library
 Evanston, Ill.
 h-lightman@northwestern.edu

Alexa Mayo
Associate Director for Services
Health Sciences and Human
    Services Library
University of Maryland, Baltimore
Baltimore, Md.
amayo@hshsl.umaryland.edu

Robert C. Michaelson
Head, Seeley G. Mudd Library for
    Science and Engineering
Northwestern University
Evanston, Ill.
rmchael@northwestern.edu

Jane Murray
Assistant Chief Librarian,
    Technical Services
Research Library
Board of Governors of the Federal
    Reserve System
Washington, D.C.
jane.e.murray@frb.gov

Anna Wu Ren
Head, Public Services
Seeley G. Mudd Library for Science
    and Engineering
Northwestern University
Evanston, Ill.
annawu@northwestern.edu

Dana L. Roth
Millikan Library
California Institute of Technology
Pasadena, Calif.
dzrlib@library.caltech.edu

Stephanie Schmitt
Supervisor, Technical Services
Library and Learning Resource
    Centre
Zayed University
Dubai, UAE
stephanie.schmitt@zu.ac.ae

Daisy Waters
Assistant Acquisitions Librarian for
    Electronic Resources
Central Technical Services
University at Buffalo (SUNY)
Buffalo, N.Y.
watersp@acsu.buffalo.edu

Printed in the United States
79672LV00002B/577-678

9 780838 984154